A Legacy Worth Sharing

Passing the Torch from One Generation of Preachers to the Next

ANDREW D. ERWIN

Charleston, AR
COBB PUBLISHING
2021

© 2021 by Andrew D. Erwin

A Legacy Worth Sharing is copyright © Andrew D. Erwin, 2021. All rights reserved. This book, either in part or the whole, is not to be duplicated, transmitted, stored, or made available in any form without the written consent of the author.

Scripture taken from the New King James Version. Copyright © 1982 by Thomas Nelson, Inc. Used by permission. All rights reserved.

ISBN: 978-1-947622-74-6

Published by:

Cobb Publishing
704 E. Main St.
Charleston, AR 72933

(479) 747-8372
www.CobbPublishing.com
CobbPublishing@gmail.com

Dedication

A Legacy Worth Sharing is the result of my doctoral dissertation on mentoring students in schools of preaching. I feel it is fitting to place the dedication page of the dissertation here, as the dedication page for the published version of the work.

In recognition of this accomplishment, I wish to express my heartfelt appreciation for the following people who have allowed, enabled, and equipped me to conduct this research project, which now concludes over twenty years of my life spent in the classroom as a student of biblical studies.

Melanie, you are the love of my life and my best friend. Without your constant encouragement, I would have quit long ago. Without you, I would not be who I am today. For you, this work is most lovingly dedicated.

To my children, Jackson, Camille, Hannah, and Emma, you bring joy to my life daily. You are a constant reminder that I made the right decision to dedicate my life to the ministry of the word. I am proud of the people you are and have confidence for your futures. To you, my babies, this research is most lovingly dedicated.

To the elders and the congregation of the West Fayetteville church of Christ, the great honor of my life is to be your preacher. You have selflessly allowed me to complete this academic endeavor and should share in a sense of accomplishment with me. Your understanding for my studies and value of me personally as a brother in Christ is heartwarming and endearing. To you, my beloved brethren, this volume is most lovingly dedicated.

I am also indebted to a few fathers in the faith. Six have now gone to be with the Lord, yet they still speak (Hebrews 11:4). Morris Bradley, Guy Hester, E. Claude Gardner, James McGill, Artie Collins, and Bill Dillon served as constant sources of encouragement and friendship. I will forever be grateful to them. These men encouraged my writing and growth as a student. Mike Kiser, Johnny Polk, and Ronald Bryant have also been constant encouragers in my life and growth as a minister of the gospel. Each of these men have been mentors to this young "Timothy," and the shepherd leadership they have provided me has truly been according to the biblical model discussed in this work. To these faithful gospel preachers, this work is lovingly dedicated.

It has taken a village of faithful and loving people to encourage me in this pursuit. As I cross the finish line, I pray that each of you know that you are crossing it with me in heart, mind, soul, and strength. I am and shall remain eternally grateful to the great God of heaven and earth for bringing each of you into my life and blessing me with the opportunity to grow in His grace and knowledge (2 Peter 3:18).

Andy Erwin

Foreword

Every successful country, company, agency, organization, people, and family is dependent on proper and perpetual mentorship. The purpose, priority, and power of mentorship in the spiritual sphere is vividly described in the apostle Paul's charge to Timothy: "Thou therefore my son, be strong in the grace that is in Christ Jesus. And the things that thou hast heard of me among many witnesses, the same commit thou to faithful men, who shall be able to teach others also" (2 Timothy 2:1-2).

The health, protection, and growth of the church today, as in every generation, is dependent upon strong and consistent mentoring of biblical principles. I can think of no area of more pressing need for written material, nor more timely subject matter than that of Biblical mentorship. There are numerous books and publications that address mentorship in a variety of areas (business, finance, athletics, etc.). However, researched, proven, and sound scripture-directed written material on spiritual mentorship has not been adequately produced, that is until now. The content of this publication has been well-researched and has produced valuable insight into the manner, means, and lasting effect that the life-on-life mentoring efforts can have on the mentor, mentee, and on the ministry process as a whole.

The author of this publication, Dr. Andy Erwin, epitomizes the desired product of sound and consistent biblical mentorship. Andy is a dedicated Bible student, a faithful minister, a skilled writer, teacher, editor, and devoted defender of truth. Brother Erwin is one of those preachers that no doubt demonstrates what the apostle Paul meant when he said, "...make full proof of thy ministry" (2 Timothy 4:5). Even with all the accomplishments he has had in his ministry, in my very first conversation with Andy, he rehearsed with me a long list of faithful men who mentored him in his Christian walk. It was therefore no surprise to me, as his dissertation chair, that when choosing as a research topic to complete his PhD degree from Amridge University, he chose to research biblical mentorship. He has earned a Doctor of Philosophy in Interdisciplinary Studies which demonstrates his commitment to study and growth. He acquired this degree not to accumulate credentials for personal acknowledgement or accolades, but to expand his ministry, and honor all those who have mentored him in that ministry.

I highly recommend the content and the author of this publication. The insight provided by brother Andy Erwin in this material will be useful to spiritual shepherds in the church, directors and faculty of preacher training schools and colleges, preachers, Bible class teachers, older Christians, younger Christians, parents, and young people. It is my hope that you will purchase, read, study, apply, and share this valuable information. To God be the Glory!

Jerry L. Martin, PhD, LPC-S

Table of Contents

Dedication 3

Foreword 5

Introduction 9

The Benefits of Mentoring Future Preachers 17

Leadership Styles in the Church 35

The Shepherd Leadership Model 49

Mentoring Preachers in the New Testament 67

Mentoring in a School of Preaching: A Case Study 79

Final Thoughts 109

Interview Questions 123

References 127

Introduction

The benefits of mentoring relationships in character formation, spiritual formation, and even ministry formation have been discussed with great enthusiasm in recent years. Mentoring is beneficial to overcoming substance abuse,[1] finishing college for first-generation college goers,[2] earning a doctoral degree,[3] increasing productivity in research as college students,[4] achieving personal and professional goals,[5] and improving workplace relations.[6]

---

[1] W.P. Williamson and Ralph W. Hood, "The Role of Mentoring in Spiritual Transformation: A Faith-Based Approach to Recovery from Substance Abuse," *Pastoral Psychology* 64, no. 1 (February 2015): 149.

[2] Veronica Fruiht and Thomas Chan, "Naturally Occurring Mentorship in a National Sample of First-Generation College Goers: A Promising Portal for Academic and Developmental Success," *American Journal of Community Psychology* 61, no. 3 (June 2018): 395.

[3] Chiyem L. Nwanzu, "Academic Programme Satisfaction and Doctorate Aspiration among Master's Degree Students: The Role of Mentoring Experience," *Ife Psychologia* 25, no. 1 (March 2017): 433–38; Jennifer Boswell, Marcella D. Stark, Angie D. Wilson, and Anthony J. Onwuegbuzie, "The Impact of Dual Roles in Mentoring Relationships: A Mixed Research Study," *Journal of Counselor Preparation and Supervision* 9, no. 2 (2017): 17–18.

[4] Julia Muschallik and Kerstin Pull, "Mentoring in Higher Education: Does It Enhance Mentees' Research Productivity?" *Education Economics* 24, no. 2 (January 1, 2016): 220; Alyse M. Anekstein and Linwood G. Vereen, "Research Mentoring: A Study of Doctoral Student Experiences and Research Productivity," *Journal of Counselor Preparation and Supervision* 11, no. 1 (2018): 21–22.

[5] Torrence E. Sparkman, "The Leadership Development Experiences of Church Denomination Executives," *The Journal of Applied Christian Leadership* 11, no. 1 (Spring 2017): 65.

[6] Nayanee Henry-Noel, Maria Bishop, Clement K. Gwede, Ekaterina Petkova, and Ewa Szumacher, "Mentorship in Medicine and Other Health Professions," *Journal of Cancer Education* 33, no. 2 (April 2018): 8.

The experience of healthy mentoring relationships also enhances one's work and life as a minister. The benefits of mentoring upon ministers include better productivity,[7] job satisfaction and longer tenure,[8] increases in leadership development,[9] avoidance of burnout,[10] and even improved physical health.[11] Some of the benefits researchers are now citing are also revealed in the Christian Scriptures.[12] God governed the children of Abraham throughout the Old Testament by designating patriarchs, prophets, priests, and kings to provide spiritual direction and guidance to Israel. God considered their failure to provide faithful guidance to His people an act of rebellion (cf. Jer. 5:30–31).

Jesus desires the same spiritual guidance for His church. In the New Testament, Christ appointed apostles to see to the

---

[7] Joshua Strunk, Frederick Milacci, and James Zabloski, "The Convergence of Ministry, Tenure, and Efficacy: Beyond Speculation Toward a New Theory of Pastoral Efficacy," *Pastoral Psychology* 66, no. 4 (August 2017): 54; Chiroma, "Mentoring as a Supportive Pedagogy," 2.

[8] Joshua Strunk, "The Convergence of Ministry, Tenure, and Efficacy," 546; Chiroma, "Mentoring as a Supportive Pedagogy," 2–3.

[9] Jeffrey S. McMaster, "The Influence of Christian Education on Leadership Development," *The Journal of Applied Christian Leadership* 7, no. 1 (Spring 2013): 73–74.

[10] Christopher J. Adams, Holly Hough, Rae Proeschold-bell, Jia Yao, and Melanie Kolkin, "Clergy Burnout: A Comparison Study with Other Helping Professions," *Pastoral Psychology* 66, no. 2 (April 2017): 167.

[11] Greg Lindholm, Judy Johnston, Frank Dong, Kim Moore, and Elizabeth Ablah, "Clergy Wellness: An Assessment of Perceived Barriers to Achieving Healthier Lifestyles," *Journal of Religion and Health* 55, no. 1 (February 2016): 102; Mark H. Anshel and Mitchell Smith, "The Role of Religious Leaders in Promoting Healthy Habits in Religious Institutions," *Journal of Religion and Health* 53, no. 4 (2014): 1046–59.

[12] For the purposes of this study, the Scriptures under consideration are those found in the Old Testament of the Hebrew Bible (39 books) and the New Testament as it is most commonly accepted (27 books).

spiritual direction and obedience of His people. The apostles understood their role as mentors and desired that this role would be perpetuated by preachers (2 Tim. 2:2), elders (1 Pet. 5:1–4), and also by older members in the congregations they established (1 Tim. 5:1, 2; Titus 2:1–8). Such spiritual direction can lead to character transformation.[13] Character transformation can also be described as moral and/or spiritual formation.[14]

In our study, the biblical shepherding model of spiritual leadership will be paired with modern mentoring theory. Emphasis will be placed upon the biblical model of shepherd leadership. With the shepherd leadership model, the leader is motivated primarily by his concern for those "sheep" who are entrusted to his care.[15] Our study confirms how the transparent and genuine affection exhibited for the Lord's people by the leader provides a truer indication of a shepherd leader than the ministry techniques utilized.[16]

The moral and spiritual transformation indicated by Paul (for example) would ideally occur through mentoring

---

[13] Chiroma, "Mentoring as a Supportive Pedagogy in Theological Training"; Mary Wanjiru Mwangi, "Perspective Transformation through Small Group Discipleship among Undergraduate University Students in Nairobi, Kenya," *Christian Education Journal* 15, no. 3 (December 2018): 345; Jean Evans, "Experience and Convergence in Spiritual Direction," *Journal of Religion and Health* 54, no. 1 (February 2015): 265.

[14] Louise Kretzschmar and Ethel C. Tuckey, "The Role of Relationship in Moral Formation: An Analysis of Three Tertiary Theological Education Institutions in South Africa," *In Die Skriflig* 51, no. 1 (2017): 5.

[15] Nathan H. Gunter, "For the Flock: Impetus for Shepherd Leadership in John 10," *The Journal of Applied Christian Leadership* 10, no. 1 (Spring 2016): 8–18.

[16] Gunter, "For the Flock," 10.

relationships between older and younger Christians. The relationship requires (1) awareness on the part of the mentors concerning the influence of their examples and their teachings; and (2) a willingness on the part of the mentees to observe and learn from these examples (cf. Acts 18:26). The same mentoring experience is evident in the relationships of Paul and Timothy and Paul and Titus. In these relationships, a preacher (Paul) acted as a mentor, even a father-figure (cf. 1 Tim. 1:2; 2 Tim. 1:2; Titus 1:4), to the other preachers.

The context for the pairing of modern mentoring theory and the shepherd model of biblical leadership is a school of preaching affiliated with a church of Christ. Since 1962, a number of churches of Christ in the United States have attempted to provide an environment consisting of mentoring relationships, spiritual direction, and ministry training to be experienced by men desiring to become ministers within this fellowship.[17] Older, experienced, and successful ministers have usually staffed these faculties to mentor and train the coming generations of ministers in an attempt to replicate the relationships found in scripture.[18]

As of 2020, there are no less than ten fulltime schools of preaching affiliated with churches of Christ in operation within the United States, with many more being conducted around the world. Usually a two-year curriculum in biblical

---

[17] Ruel Lemmons, "The Training of Gospel Preachers," *Firm Foundation* 82, no. 27 (July 1965): 418; Robert S. Bell, "An Elder's Charge," *Firm Foundation* 96, no. 4 (January 79): 52.

[18] Ruel Lemmons, "Bear Valley Opens School of Preaching," *Firm Foundation* 82, no. 27 (July 1965): 427; Alan E. Highers, "Getwell Road School of Preaching," *Gospel Advocate* 108, no. 5 (February 1966): 68.

textual studies and ministry courses is offered. Some schools are now providing graduate courses and degrees.[19]

The purpose for beginning the schools included the following reasons: (1) to equip ministers with a sound biblical education and skills necessary to be successful in ministry; (2) to offer said education without the debt usually associated with Christian colleges (i.e. tuition, room and board, etc.); (3) to allow established veteran ministers to mentor future ministers; and (4) to meet the growing need for ministers in churches of Christ.[20]

Churches of Christ which operate these schools do so intending to provide other churches of Christ with ministers who are both theologically grounded as well as capable of putting into practice what they learn.[21] Our study also confirms that theological education when supported by the mentoring experience has the potential of bridging the gap between the theory of moral and spiritual formation and the actual practice of helping another to achieve it.[22]

We will see that the viability of these schools of preaching to offer suitable ministerial training depends upon their awareness and ability to provide a biblical mentoring experience to their students. Many physical, mental, and spiritual benefits are to be derived from healthy mentoring

---

[19] The curriculum and design of each school can generally be accessed from the school's catalog on the respective websites.

[20] Roy J. Hearn, "Getwell Road School of Preaching," *Gospel Advocate* 110, no. 5 (February 1968): 68.

[21] Roy J. Hearn, "Wanted: Men Who Are Not Afraid of Hard Work," *First Century Christian* 1, no. 4 (October 1967): 9-10.

[22] Kretzschmar, "The Role of Relationship," 5.

practices.[23] By examining the biblical nature of the mentoring practices that are experienced by students within a school of preaching operated by a church of Christ, we will discover the derived benefits and/or possible pitfalls to be avoided.

Schools of preaching have a powerful influence on churches of Christ throughout the world and represent an educational model unique to this fellowship.[24] In many regards the concept of schools of preaching is still in its beginning stages as new schools emerge and existing schools continue to attract "a considerable portion of the potential ministers, leaders, and donors within Churches of Christ."[25] Yet, "scholarly literature surrounding them is disturbingly scarce."[26] Moreover, the issue of the retention in ministry of the graduates of these schools remains a critical issue in need of further study[27] and is one of the issues discussed in this study.

We will also examine the different types of mentoring relationships and practices that have been present during the

---

[23] Henry-Noel, 3.

[24] Matthew Emile Vaughan, "On Schools of Preaching," *Journal of Faith and Academy* 5, no. 1 (Spring 2012): 61.

[25] Matthew Emile Vaughan, "On Schools of Preaching," 61.

[26] Vaughan, 61. Vaughan notes, "Mention of these institutions is even absent from many of the standard texts dealing with the SCM." (Stone-Campbell Movement, ADE) He cites the works of Leroy Garrett and Richard Hughes as examples. One outdated work is also cited by Vaughan. It is Jim Harris' work, *Schools of Preaching: An Evaluation of Ministry Preparation* (Fort Worth, TX: Star Bible, 1984). Harris did note that at that time over 5,000 students had graduated from schools of preaching, 36.

[27] Vaughan, 73. Again, for lack of fresh material, Vaughan was forced to cited Harris' work wherein Harris argued that in 1984 only about 50% of the graduates of the schools of preaching remained in fulltime pulpit ministry after their first employment. Harris, 37–9.

students' educational experiences. Mentoring practices are diverse. Mentoring can be formal, planned, and structured. It can also be informal with relationships which naturally occur. The form of mentorship can be dyadic, multiple, apprentice, or team.[28] The method of delivery can be through peer mentoring, senior mentoring, and distance or virtual mentoring.[29]

We will also seek to prove the benefits of the mentoring experiences for the students in their respective ministries after graduation. The benefits of the biblical mentoring experience are not to be enjoyed exclusively by the student while engaging the rigors of academic exercises, but also by the people he serves in his evangelistic ministry. Our findings show that the biblical mentoring experience can influence the mentee in a positive way so that he can likewise be a positive influence for others.

---

[28] Henry-Noel, "Mentorship in Medicine and Other Health Professions," 3.
[29] Henry-Noel, 3.

Chapter One

The Benefits of Mentoring Future Preachers

The experience of healthy mentoring relationships enhances one's life and work as a minister with benefits which include better productivity, job satisfaction, longer tenure,[1] increases in leadership development,[2] avoidance of burnout,[3] and even improved physical health.[4] A mentor-mentee relationship in theological education and ministry formation is extremely valuable, as was indicated by a survey conducted by the Fuller Theological Seminary's School of Psychology.[5] The study revealed that only 20% of their graduates from seminary were active in ministry after ten years.[6] One of the key factors for the 20% who remained in ministry was having a mentoring experience while at the Fuller Theological Seminary; which even continued after their seminary training.[7] Students who have been mentored while in school also tend to have a better grasp of controversial issues in ministry, conflict management, and sermon

---

[1] Strunk, "The Convergence of Ministry," 541; Chiroma, "Mentoring," 2.
[2] McMaster, "The Influence of Christian Education," 73–4.
[3] Adams, "Clergy Burnout: A Comparison Study," 167.
[4] Lindholm, "Clergy Wellness: An Assessment," 102; Anshel, "The Role of Religious Leaders," 1046–59.
[5] Chiroma, "Mentoring," 2
[6] Chiroma, 2.
[7] Chiroma, 2.

preparation and delivery, which, in turn, helps prepare them for their work in ministry.[8]

Spiritual Formation and Moral Formation

The term "spiritual formation" is used, especially in the theological and ministerial context, to describe building depth, commitment, and active faith.[9] Spiritual formation can be equated with the process of transformation spoken of by Paul (Rom. 12:1, 2; Eph. 4:23), in which the mind is renewed and the character of the individual is transformed into the character of Christ. Moral formation involves growth in knowing, being, and doing, which together lead to moral relationships, moral living, and the flourishing of humans and all creation in harmony with God.[10] Such formation requires community both at the conceptual and practical levels and the teaching, training, and encouragement that only a moral community can provide.[11]

The goal of such spiritual and moral formation is Christian virtue. Christian virtue can be described as having godly excellence, godly goodness, and godly righteousness.[12] It is the application of a conscious will to do what is right from God's revealed Word and from personal responsibility.[13] It encompasses integrity, honesty, modesty, and purity.[14] Virtue

---

[8] Strunk, "The Convergence of Ministry," 537–50.
[9] Chiroma, "Mentoring," 4.
[10] Kretzschmar, "The Role of Relationship in Moral Formation," 3.
[11] Kretzschmar, 3.
[12] Kretzschmar, 3.
[13] Kretzschmar, 3.
[14] Kretzschmar, 3.

not only serves as a guide for our daily lives or decisions but also helps us give the best of ourselves.[15]

Nathan Chiroma and Anita Cloete examined the mentoring programs in three Evangelical Church Winning All (ECWA) seminaries in Nigeria. They determined that when theological training was coupled with effective mentoring, the spiritual growth, character development, and ministry formation of the theological students was enhanced.[16] In order for a theological education to be complete, more than the mere transfer of information must occur.[17] Theological students need role models to provide Christian examples and mentoring relationships to direct them within their educational community.[18]

Theological education can tend to concentrate almost solely on imparting knowledge.[19] Yet, the professional skills and especially the moral formation required for ministry are too important to overlook.[20] Theological education when supported by the mentoring experience has the potential of bridging the gap between theory and practice.[21] However, a need for improvement and deliberate focus remains.[22]

Seminaries can be slow to incorporate actual mentoring programs even after including them in the curriculum.[23] An

---

[15] Kretzschmar, 3.
[16] Chiroma, "Mentoring," 1.
[17] Chiroma, 3.
[18] Chiroma, 3.
[19] Kretzschmar, "The Role of Relationship," 1.
[20] Kretzschmar, 1.
[21] Kretzschmar, 5.
[22] Kretzschmar, 5.
[23] Kretzschmar, 2.

initial survey of the websites and catalogs of ten fulltime schools of preaching operated by churches of Christ in the United States concur with these findings, as only two schools mentioned mentoring experiences/programs specifically.[24]

Kretzschmar and Tuckey studied the role of relationship and moral formation in three separate theological institutions in South Africa.[25] The constant thread that ran throughout the responses of the students to their questionnaire was *relationship*.[26] Modes of moral formation involving relationships with God, self, and others had the greatest influence on students' moral formation.[27] Finding ways to foster relationships between staff and students and between fellow students was a key to the moral formation of the students.[28]

Fostering these relationships in schools of theology requires a conscious and systematic implementation of such practices as mentoring, tutoring, and group discussions. These efforts can build self-esteem and emotional awareness.[29] When properly organized and conscientiously maintained as a supportive pedagogy in theological education, mentoring can

---

[24] The schools which specifically mentioned an ongoing mentoring program were Bear Valley Bible Institute in Denver, Colorado, and the Brown Trail School of Preaching in Bedford, Texas. Other schools provide opportunities where mentoring could occur, but "mentoring programs" as such were not mentioned.
[25] Kretzschmar, "The Role of Relationship."
[26] Kretzschmar, 6.
[27] Kretzschmar, 8.
[28] Kretzschmar, 7.
[29] Kretzschmar, 7.

provide an opportunity to address personal development issues essential to success in local church ministry.[30]

One possible design for a mentoring program requires a mentor being assigned to each student during the first semester of admittance.[31] The mentor is to establish a continuous student-mentor relationship with the student throughout his or her seminary experience.[32] However, one of the greatest possible obstacles to effective mentoring in theological education is that a mentor could be overworked.[33] A teacher's workload could be especially problematic in a school of preaching where the faculties are considerably smaller.

An organized mentoring program will also require theological schools to provide teachers/mentors with continuous training in mentoring principles and skills.[34] Such training would need to be comprehensive and on-going throughout their involvement in the program.[35] Faculty members who are expected to serve as mentors will need to be provided the resources required to carry out the task of mentoring students.[36] Resource materials and financial support would have to be provided to help them understand and fulfil their responsibilities as mentors.[37]

---

[30] Chiroma, "Mentoring," 4.
[31] Chiroma, 6.
[32] Chiroma, 6.
[33] Chiroma, 6.
[34] Chiroma, 6.
[35] Chiroma, 6.
[36] Chiroma, 6.
[37] Chiroma, 6.

A similar study was conducted by Mwangi, which found transformational pedagogy was of primary importance.[38] Students in the undergraduate university discipleship ministry under LIFE Ministry Kenya (Campus Crusade for Christ) within Nairobi provided the target populace.[39] Five themes represented a combination of the contributing factors as to how perspective transformation was fostered through small-group discipleship in that school.[40] *Mentoring* was the term which came up often in the findings, as participants in this study spoke of their transformative experiences through discipleship. Participants repeatedly referred to their small group leader as their mentor. They talked extensively about how helpful it was for them to have someone walk with them as they learned about discipleship and made various adjustments in their ways of life.[41]

The two functions mentors provided that were believed to be the most significant to the students' transformative process were *guidance* and *dialogue*. Thirteen of the sixteen students identified being given guidance as one of the most important roles the mentors played in their lives.[42] The students' transformative process was also impacted through dialogue for relationship building and also for sharing thoughts and experiences.[43] Participants believed their

---

[38] Mwangi, "Perspective Transformation," 345.
[39] Mwangi, 344.
[40] Mwangi, 345.
[41] Mwangi, 352.
[42] Mwangi, 352.
[43] Mwangi, 353.

leader's role of guiding and engaging dialogue was important to their transformation.[44]

The importance of the role of the mentoring relationship in the context of transformational development was not limited to the classroom. Students were also given the opportunity to observe their mentors modeling how to do ministry, which further strengthened their skill acquisition.[45]

White and Afrane provide an additional study from the context of Christian universities in Africa, specifically in Ghana.[46] The realities and challenges of maintaining Christian virtues and ethos were examined with possible solutions being recommended.[47] The study unearthed some of the major factors affecting the maintenance of Christian virtues and ethos in these universities in Ghana. The issues discussed include secularism, modernity, increase in student population, and the challenge of finding qualified Christians for various positions.[48] It should be noted that Christian schools in the United States face these same issues. With erudite clarity these scholars have also stated what it means to be a "Christian university" and challenged others in the process. Observe:

> It is not enough to claim to be a Christian university. A university being founded by a church does not mean that it is a Christian university. A university having the word

---

[44] Mwangi, 353.
[45] Mwangi, 357.
[46] White, "Maintaining Christian Virtues and Ethos," 1–8.
[47] White.
[48] White.

'Christian' or the name 'Christ' as part of their name or vision and mission statement does not make it a Christian university. What we should not forget is that there is evidence of universities that started with clear Christian philosophies of education and commitment to sound doctrine but have over time abandoned their commitment to the basic tenets of the faith.

The writers provide a basic definition and forthright plea for Christian universities, stating,

> What defines a university as a Christian university is that, it must be Christ-centred, mission-minded and discipleship focused. These three attributes are in line with the great commission and are the basic principles that will transform the lives of the enrolled students. It also helps them to see their academic training as an opportunity to develop their capacities to become agents of transformation and ambassadors of Christ. It gives students the confidence and assurance that their future is secured. To be Christ-centred means to see Jesus Christ as the centre of every activity that goes on in the university. This includes the academic, administrative and spiritual lives of the staff and students of the university.[49]

Primary data was collected through questionnaires administered to students, lecturers, and senior administrators of three private Christian university colleges in Ghana (Christian Service University College; Pentecost University College; and Methodist University College). A need was

---

[49] White, 2–3.

discovered for both students and staff in these Christian schools to have a holistic Christocentric approach to teaching and learning.[50]

The desired approach to learning was made possible when Christian principles and virtues were integrated into academic programs and curriculums of the universities.[51] Mentoring programs, chaplains, and required chapel services proved to be valuable resources when the spiritual maturity of the facilitators are thoughtfully considered.[52] However, mentoring programs alone were insufficient to maintain Christian virtues and ethos on campus when a Bible-based curriculum was lacking.[53]

Teachers who integrate biblical principles in their lectures and present themselves as Christians to a high extent are most effective as role-models.[54] The effectiveness of mentoring practices in a Christian school, more specifically, a school which has been established for the training of Christian ministers, in the context of an ever-increasing secular environment, depends on the integration of Christian faith, principles, and virtues.[55]

The four articles reviewed arrive at a singular conclusion: character and moral formation best occur in Christian universities when academics are supported by effective

---

[50] White, 2–3.
[51] White, 4.
[52] White, 8.
[53] White, 8.
[54] White, 8.
[55] White, 1.

mentoring[56] that is both conscious and systematic.[57] As relationships are developed, teachers serving as mentors deliberately become involved with their students as individuals and find ways to strengthen their faith and spiritual development beyond the classroom. Schools accomplish their desired goal by providing a setting or program in which the mentoring experience can thrive and wherein comprehensive orientation and training for mentors is provided.[58]

Authentic Leadership Qualities

Authentic leadership is a quality which can be developed in all individuals.[59] Relational transparency is a key component of authentic leadership.[60] Relationships are at the heart of the mentoring experience and encourage spiritual and moral formation.[61] Authentic leadership is genuine and honest. It is conveyed through an internalized moral perspective, self-awareness, and with balanced processing.[62] The benefits of authentic leadership include confidence, hope, optimism, and resiliency.[63]

The positive effects of a mentoring relationship have also been observed by researchers in the context of leadership in

---

[56] Chiroma, "Mentoring," 1.
[57] Kretzschmar, "The Role of Relationship," 8.
[58] Kretzschmar, 8.
[59] Timothy R. Puls, Laverne L. Ludden, and James Freemyer, "Authentic Leadership and Its Relationship to Ministerial Effectiveness," *The Journal of Applied Christian Leadership* 8, no. 1 (Spring 2014): 56.
[60] Puls, "Authentic Leadership," 56.
[61] Kretzschmar, "The Role of Relationship," 6.
[62] Puls, "Authentic Leadership," 56.
[63] Puls, 56.

the church setting.[64] Sparkman took a phenomenological approach[65] to understand the leadership development of eight jurisdictional bishops of a predominately African American denomination with an ecclesiastical structure.[66] Each one stated that the benefits of "experiential relationships" with mentors[67] helped them to establish standards of faith and values.[68] Each one of these bishops also had a prior relationship with a jurisdictional bishop who provided an opportunity to see the jurisdictional office at work, could help shape their future, saw their potential, and pushed them to achieve.[69]

Sparkman's findings concur with those of McMaster. McMaster studied the influence of mentoring in Christian education (K-12) upon leadership development.[70] He found an interesting dichotomy resulting from his surveys. Sometimes the mentoring was intentional (formal) and sometimes it was unintentional (informal).[71] The mentoring occurred in a variety of ways, but always in a relational manner.[72] The teachers best mentored when demonstrating compassion and personal interest, intentionally seeking to shape and influence students through personal interactions.[73] Once again, the concept of *relationship* was at the heart of the mentoring

---

[64] Sparkman, "The Leadership Development Experiences," 61.
[65] Sparkman, 61.
[66] Sparkman, 55
[67] Sparkman, 62–4.
[68] Sparkman, 63.
[69] Sparkman, 65.
[70] McMaster, "The Influence of Christian Education," 73.
[71] McMaster, 73.
[72] McMaster, 73.
[73] McMaster, 73.

process and leadership development, especially during the high school years.

McMaster's participants believed the educational environment to be one that provided and facilitated the development of those important relationships.[74] He suggests that Christian schools can enhance their efforts on leadership through relationship and biblical integration.[75] Faculty and staff can be taught effective relational mentoring skills, and school leadership can foster a work environment that allows for and encourages this activity.[76] The integration of biblical learning, role models of the Christian faith, and the act of challenging a student to think through his beliefs throughout the educational experience proved to be most effective.[77]

Authentic leadership qualities are also key components to the success of a minister. A study was conducted in which the researchers examined the authentic leadership traits of clergy and discovered significant relationships of predictability as well as positive correlations with ministerial effectiveness.[78] A survey was conducted of 58 experienced ordained pastors of the Indiana District of the Lutheran church (Missouri Synod) and 164 of their lay leaders that indicated a significant relationship between authentic leadership and ministerial effectiveness.[79] The way in which these ministers transparently related to and built trust with leaders in their

---

[74] McMaster, 75.
[75] McMaster, 81.
[76] McMaster, 81.
[77] McMaster, 81.
[78] Puls, "Authentic Leadership," 55.
[79] Puls, 55.

respective congregations was crucial to the development of trust and a willingness to invest in the future mission of the congregation.[80]

As a result of their findings, the researchers warned against the traditional seminary curriculum. Traditionally, seminaries have tended to focus more on preaching, ministry, and biblical education, while oftentimes failing to develop a functional understanding leadership behavior in the student. Such a curriculum may in fact be hampering the retention of ministers in active ministry, resulting in burnout if and when expectations are unrealized.[81] Hence, they called for a renewal of authentic leadership as a critical component of pastoral leadership and as a response to the gap between expectations and reality.[82]

Scholars are seeing the need for ministers to have authentic leadership qualities in order to have a viable ministry.[83] Leadership qualities can be adapted through the mentoring experience. If schools of theological and ministerial training will incorporate mentoring programs and mentorship training into their respective programs, the prospects for greater leadership development will be enhanced. Thus, by implementing a structured mentoring program, schools can encourage spiritual and character formation, while also developing sound leadership characteristics in their students.

---

[80] Puls, 67.
[81] Puls, 69.
[82] Puls, 69.
[83] E.g., Chiroma, "Mentoring," Strunk, "The Convergence of Ministry," Kretzschmar, "the Role of Relationship," and Puls.

Tenure and Efficacy in Ministry

Defining ministerial efficacy can often become an arbitrary and subjective exercise. Recent studies conducted by Strunk, Milacci, and Zabloski[84] have helped to provide a more objective understanding for ministerial efficacy. By studying the experiences of long-tenured (i.e., more than six years with a congregation) ministers in Christian churches,[85] the researchers found that the participants realized that ministry, tenure, and efficacy converged through faithfulness to their calling and authenticity in their church community.[86] A basis for a new theory of pastoral efficacy has been established through their work.[87] Realizing that a minister's efficacy cannot always be defined by the numerical growth of the congregation he serves,[88] these participants understood that a minister's efficacy can also be evaluated by faithfulness to his calling[89] and by spiritual growth and transformation in the lives of the respective congregations.[90]

The effectiveness of a minister and his work cannot be quantified solely on the numerical growth of the congregation he serves. Within churches of Christ in the United States this is especially true, as churches which are growing numerically are the exception rather than the norm.[91] Ministers who are

---

[84] Strunk, "The Convergence of Ministry."
[85] Strunk, 537.
[86] Strunk, 537.
[87] Strunk, 537.
[88] Strunk, 538.
[89] Strunk, 541.
[90] Strunk, 542.
[91] Carl Royster, *Churches of Christ in the United States* (Nashville, TN: 21st Century Christian, 2018), 21.

agents of spiritual transformation (cf. Rom. 12:1, 2) should be valued as being effective in their respective ministries.[92]

Three questions were asked by Strunk, et al: (1) how do long-tenured senior pastors describe their experience of being long tenured? (2) In what ways do long-tenured senior pastors perceive that their education prepared them for a long tenure? (3) In addition to pastoral education, what other dynamics do long-tenured senior pastors perceive as contributing to their long tenure?[93] They found three commonalities within the context of the participants' faith journeys: (1) the influence of mentors, (2) experiences of adversity, and (3) awareness of their own needs.[94] The participants stated that mentoring relationships in their lives had helped to shape their thinking about what it means to be a pastor and to do the work of pastoral ministry.[95]

Again, the researchers recommend a re-thinking and restructuring of curricula and instruction in theological institutions where students are being trained for ministry. Pastoral education can facilitate the development of the study and understanding of theology as well a practical philosophy of ministry.[96] In addition to biblical and theological studies, and the emphasis on leadership and management, the study calls for a greater emphasis to be placed on self-care, cultural

---

[92] Strunk, "Convergence," 542.
[93] Strunk, 538.
[94] Strunk, 541.
[95] Strunk, 541.
[96] Strunk, 541.

and emotional intelligence, and the health of marriage and family.[97]

The findings and recommendations of this study agree with the findings and recommendations of other studies.[98] The findings also concur with studies related to clergy burnout, as researchers have found that clergy burnout can be avoided through healthy mentoring relationships.[99] Naturally, if a minister's tenure can be lengthened in part due to healthy mentoring relationships, burnout and compassion fatigue would also be lessened.

Implications from Other Studies

The positive effects of the mentoring relationship have been studied in other areas besides ministry. While these studies have been conducted in other fields, the implications to the mentor/ministry dynamic can be explored. For example, mentors can have a positive influence on students finishing and continuing their education.[100] Positive results have also been found in counselor education, especially when teachers had dual roles of teacher and mentor.[101] Counselor education programs can facilitate such relationships by

---

[97] Strunk, 541.

[98] The findings and recommendations from this research also concur with previous studies beyond the time restraints of this review. See Elisabeth H. Selzer, "Effectiveness of a Seminary's Training and Mentoring Program and Subsequent Job Satisfaction of Its Graduates," *Journal of Research on Christian Education* 17, no. 1 (January 2008): 35.

[99] Adams, "Clergy Burnout: A Comparison Study," 167; Barnard, "The Relationship of Clergy Burnout," 151.

[100] Nwanzu, "Academic Programme Satisfaction," 433–8; Boswell, "The Impact of Dual Roles,"17–18.

[101] Boswell, "Impact," 1–27.

strategically assigning advisees, teaching assistants, and research assistants.[102] Benefits of an actual research mentor role for doctoral students were also uncovered.[103] The findings concur with the findings we have noted previously.[104] An increase in productivity on the part of the student has also resulted from the mentoring experience.[105]

Another study, however, has found a significant distinction in the productivity of students who had a formal mentoring experience as compared to those who had an informal mentoring experience.[106] Schools which implemented a formal/structured mentoring program to provide a mentoring experience were more effective in encouraging productivity among students, as well as providing encouragement to further their studies in other institutions.[107]

Conclusion

The mentoring relationship can have a positive effect upon one's spiritual and physical health.[108] The benefits of the mentoring experience among ministers is simply too great for the practice to be neglected in schools where future ministers are trained. While several seminaries have included mentoring programs, the actual practice of mentoring has not

---

[102] Boswell, 18.
[103] Boswell, 18.
[104] E.g., Chiroma, "Mentoring," Kretzschmar, "The Role of Mentoring," Puls, "Authentic Leadership"
[105] Anekstein, "Research Mentoring," 1–28.
[106] Muschallik, "Mentoring in Higher Education" 210–23.
[107] Muschallik.
[108] Lindholm, "Clergy Wellness," 97–109.

always been sufficiently developed.[109] When formal mentoring practices are employed, the benefits are numerous. The school undertaking the task of training ministers will do well to consider its mentoring practices.

Character transformation, improved leadership skills, efficacy, and tenure are each positively affected through the mentoring experience. We have a worthwhile study for a worthwhile cause. The preaching of the gospel is too important for schools intending to train ministers not to do everything possible to ensure the effectiveness of the training given to those who would so dedicate their lives.

---

[109] Kretzschmar, "Relationship," 2.

Chapter Two

Leadership Styles in the Church

Schools of preaching that are operated by churches of Christ are unique in theological education and ministerial training in that they are works overseen by the various congregations that operate them. As such, these schools are accountable to the elders of their respective congregations, just as are the people who comprise the congregations.

The church leaders are responsible for the overall operation of the school, rather than a board of directors, trustees, or executive officers. Thus, the subject of church leadership is of vital importance to the mentoring experiences of the students in these institutions.

Researchers in the field of practical theology have long recognized that church leaders cannot effectively and consistently function without an overall theory, interpretation, or model of leadership.[1] It is important to recognize which (if any) of the prevalent leadership models adheres most to the biblical model of church leadership and,

---

[1] Robert D. Dale, *Seeds for the Future: Growing Organic Leaders for Living Churches* (St. Louis, MO: Lake Hickory Resources, 2005), 19. One of the esteemed scholars among churches of Christ in the field of church leadership, Norman Hogan, would refer to ineffective leadership as the "scourge of the local church." Norman Hogan, *Leadership in the Local Church* (Henderson, TN: Hester Publications, 1988), 5. While it has been thirty years since Hogan's book was first published, it helps to establish the pattern of teaching among churches of Christ in regard to the importance of leadership models from Hogan (1988), to Fair (2008), to Shepherd (2018).

therefore, is most conducive to the biblical mentoring experience.

The Directive Style

One mode of leadership is the *manager* or *directive* style of leadership.[2] In the context of church leadership, the manger functions similarly to the corporate style often found in the secular world. In some instances, the directive style is characterized by elders who act as administrators. Directives are handed down from the hierarchy (the church leaders, or elders) to the organization (the church).[3] The bottom line, rather than relationship building becomes the central focus. Motivation is offered through facts, goals, and tasks to be met.[4] Success is viewed in terms of the size of the budget and the condition of the property, with primary attention being given to the number of adherents to the services of the church.[5]

Directive leadership also includes the direct and personal involvement of the leader.[6] Such "managers" tend to believe that to be good leaders they must have control of everything within the organization,[7] including determining the vision, direction, and goals of the organization.[8] The directive model

---

[2] Ian A. Fair, *Leadership in the Kingdom: Sensitive Strategies for the Church in a Changing World* (Abilene, TX: ACU Press, 2008), 59–60.

[3] Roger E. Shepherd, *Church Growth and Membership Involvement in a Contemporary Community* (Montgomery, AL: Amridge University Press, 2018), 89–90.

[4] Fair, *Leadership in the Kingdom*, 108.

[5] Shepherd, *Church Growth and Membership Involvement*, 93.

[6] Fair, *Leadership*, 108.

[7] Shepherd, *Church Growth*, 95.

[8] Fair, 108.

can also give the appearance that the interests or expertise of the leader or leadership team are more essential to the health and growth of the organization than the combined ability, knowledge, or interests of the organization.[9] The tendency is to create a love-hate dichotomy within the group.[10] People who have a strong self-image will usually leave the group because of the frustration created by what is perceived to be the excessive control of a directive leadership.[11] The effects of this management style can be catastrophic to the organization. Fair cites frustration, resentment, apathy, and lethargy among the possible negative consequences.[12]

Within the setting of a school of preaching, a directive form of leadership could manifest similar tendencies. If the school's success is to be measured by the size of enrollment, the condition of the facilities, and other similar physical assets, what importance would be placed on the quality and preparedness of the student being graduated from the school? If the church's leaders had direct control in the daily operations of the school, as well as in determining the vision, goals, and tasks of the school, would it not be difficult to employ a director or faculty members who possess a strong self-image?

However, benefits can also be derived from other characteristics of the directive form of leadership. For example, controversies could develop within the school which

---

[9] Fair, 107
[10] Fair, 108.
[11] Fair, 108.
[12] Fair, 109.

would require a strong, aggressive leadership to settle them. Moreover, some students who need structure and control in their lives may enroll in a school because of its strong directive leadership, finding direction in the goals and vision provided.[13]

The Political Style

A second possible method for church leadership is the *political* method. Fair refers to this as the *"democratic"* model.[14] Such a style is evident when the organization is led through a political process characterized by negotiation, compromise, and consensus for decision making.[15] Changes tend to occur seldom or slowly at best with such a manner of leadership.

The political or democratic model frequently exists in congregations which do not have elders to lead. In the missional context, the political model is quite prevalent as no other effective leadership core usually exists.[16] The democratic style of leadership can also appear in congregations which lack strong and decisive leaders among the elders. When elders are uncertain or afraid of how their decisions will be received by the congregation, the political/democratic style becomes apparent. One of the greatest weaknesses of this style of leadership appears when the uninformed or less mature have the power to overrule the experienced, more mature members of the group through

---
[13] Fair, 108.
[14] Fair, 109.
[15] Fair, 109–10.
[16] Fair, 111.

a majority vote.[17] As a result, the political style of leadership can lead to self-interest, personal competition, power struggles, and ultimately division within the group.[18]

Within the setting of a school of preaching, the church's leadership could seek a consensus among the administration and possibly the faculty to facilitate the needs for the daily operation of the school. The direction, vision, and goals of the school could also be a matter of consensus. Such a situation would seem to be very favorable for the functioning of the school as long as the leadership team was comprised of faithful, informed, and mature Christians.

What influence might this style of leadership have on the mentoring experiences of the students? Fair notes, "There is a narrow line separating democratic leadership style and participative leadership style."[19] The participative model is most likely to be found in organizations which indicate no major differences between the expertise, maturity, goals, and vision of the leaders and the workers.[20] Participatory leaders initiate the process of decision making and empower the group to work freely within the established values and organizational parameters.[21] Ministry leaders equip the group for ministry by seeking to develop the passions and skills of the group.

---

[17] Fair, 110.
[18] Fair, 110.
[19] Fair, 111.
[20] Fair, 111.
[21] Fair, 111.

Collaborative Style

Hartwig and Bird refer to a similar model of leadership as *collaborative* or *shared* leadership, recommending that ministry teams be formed and empowered with the authority to provide direction for the particular aspect of ministry they are given.[22] Fair's participative model for leadership is very similar to Hartwig and Bird's collaborative model. In the participatory model, the leaders initiate the process of decision making and empower the group. Leaders are to lead by example and creative initiative.[23] A slight difference occurs in the collaborative process – the group provides the direction for itself, sometimes through democratic means. Thus, the group leads the group. Some scholars also combine elements of both models into what is to be deemed the disciple-led or servant-led leadership model.[24]

Robert Dale recognizes the need for leaders in the church or in ministry teams to realize the potential leadership qualities in others and to begin cultivating the "organic growth" of new leaders through time, patience, and the participatory process.[25] Dale urges present-day leaders to be future oriented and to consider their roles as that of caretakers.[26] He urges leaders to mentor prospective leaders,

---

[22] Ryan T. Hartwig and Warren Bird, *Teams that Thrive: Five Disciplines of Collaborative Church Leadership* (Downers Grove, IL: Inter-Varsity Press, 2015).

[23] Fair, 111.

[24] Dale L. Lemke, "The Philosophy of Disciple-Centered Leadership," *Christian Education Journal* 14, no. 2 (2017): 271–284.

[25] Dale, *Seeds for the Future*, 26.

[26] Dale, 138.

and to collaborate with them in planning and establishing goals.[27]

Dale also calls for every member to be involved in setting goals for the organization. He states, "The deeper and broader the ownership of organizational goals, the more likely members are to trust the leaders and the formal structures."[28] Furthermore, "Healthy congregations do not depend solely on pastors or leader teams for their kingdom dream...the entire congregation is responsible for church management."[29] According to Dale's understanding of this model, leaders are simply in place to guide and maintain the congregation's dream and ministry.[30]

Regarding the training of preachers, Bushfield recognizes the value of the collaborative model in the mentoring experience. He states, "Teachers of preaching need to equip students with a set of tools and a framework for continuing to learn as they head out into life and ministry."[31] Moreover, homiletic teachers can encourage future preachers by "casting a vision for the centrality of preaching and the importance of doing it well [and]...direct students toward taking additional preaching electives while still in school to build an even stronger foundation for future ministry and

---

[27] Dale, 9.
[28] Robert D. Dale, *To Dream Again, Again* (Macon, GA: Nurturing Faith, Inc., 2018), 83.
[29] Dale, *To Dream Again*, 101.
[30] Dale, 101.
[31] Timothy Bushfield, "Teaching with Trajectory: Equipping Students for the Lifelong Journey of Learning to Preach," in *Training Preachers: A Guide to Teaching Homiletics*, ed. Scott M. Gibson (Bellingham, WA: Lexham Press, 2018), 169.

learning."[32] Bushfield calls for "collaborative homiletics" wherein preachers could partner with members of their congregations to address the preparation, delivery, and evaluation of sermons.[33]

A collaborative approach to preaching could enhance the mentoring experiences of students in a school of preaching if it were employed. Perhaps this method could be implemented by including members of the church's leadership, faculty from the school, and/or members of the student body. Or, perhaps this method could be utilized with a single teacher serving as a mentor to a single preaching student.

The collaborative theory has plausible reasons for consideration in the field of ministry training. History provides us with a successful record of ministers who collaborated with would-be ministers utilizing an "apprenticeship approach" in ministry training. Gibson notes, "From the early church [in America] onward, apprenticeship of ministers formed the practice of developing leadership for the local church."[34] Nathanael Emmons was one such preacher who used the apprenticeship approach to training preachers in eighteenth century New England. He has been remembered for his mentoring in homiletics, giving special advice on sermon construction, public speaking, matters of style and delivery, and influencing sermon construction in New England for half a

---

[32] Bushfield, "Teaching with Trajectory," 177.
[33] Bushfield, 180.
[34] Scott M. Gibson, "The Place of Preaching Professors in Theological Education," in *Training Preachers: A Guide to Teaching Homiletics*, ed. Scott M. Gibson (Bellingham, WA: Lexham Press, 2018), 11.

century.[35] So effective was the apprenticeship approach that it remained a model for training preachers long after theological seminaries were established in the United States.[36]

The apprenticeship approach to ministerial training has also been used with great success within churches of Christ in the United States. In the nineteenth century, T. B. Larimore mentored many of his preaching students at his Mars Hill College in Florence, Alabama.[37] The apprenticeship approach was taken with young preachers, especially during their summer vacation from school.[38] Larimore and "his boys" spent many weeks together preaching throughout the rural communities of northwest Alabama.[39] Larimore not only taught his students about preaching and sermon development, but also about the importance of doctrine, compassion in ministry, and pious Christian manhood.[40]

During the twentieth century it became a frequent practice of churches to employ a younger preacher to serve as an apprentice to be mentored by an older preacher. Gus Nichols mentored many young preachers in this way while serving the Sixth Avenue church in Jasper, Alabama.[41] Not only did Gus

---

[35] Mary Latimer Gambrell, *Ministerial Training in Eighteenth-Century New England* (New York: AMS, 1967), 126.
[36] Gibson, "The Place of Preaching Professors," 14.
[37] F.D. Srygley, *Larimore and His Boys* (Nashville, TN: Gospel Advocate Co., 1955).
[38] Srygley, *Larimore and His Boys*, 140.
[39] Srygley, 145 ff.
[40] Srygley, 131, 226, 248, 256, 281.
[41] Scott Harp, *The Sage of Jasper: Gus Nichols, A Biography* (Charleston, AR: Cobb Publishing, 2019), 416–20.

Nichols use his time to help young "associate" ministers, but he also mentored preachers from as far away as Tennessee and Mississippi during special Friday-night and Saturday-morning preacher-training classes.[42]

Among African American evangelists, Marshall Keeble employed the apprenticeship method most effectively. He was not fixed in a local ministry at one specific place but held evangelistic meetings throughout the country and as far away as Nigeria. Marshall Keeble would have his "spiritual sons" travel with him and even preach during many of these meetings. A biographer of Keeble, Edward J. Robinson, attributes much of the credit for founding and strengthening African American churches of Christ across the New South and beyond to Keeble and his spiritual sons, noting his preaching ability, leadership skills, and magnetic personality.[43] Robinson writes

> Marshall Keeble's greatest legacy may well have been the company of spiritual sons he left behind who perpetuated his work of planting, edifying, and solidifying black Churches of Christ throughout the South. African American Churches of Christ owed their rise not only to the efforts of Keeble, but also to the indefatigable corps of young men whom Keeble baptized, instructed, and charged with an evangelistic mission.[44]

---

[42] Harp, 337–8.

[43] Edward J. Robinson, *Show Us How You Do It: Marshall Keeble and the rise of Black Churches of Christ in the United States, 1914-1968* (Tuscaloosa, AL: University of Alabama Press, 2008), 154.

[44] Robinson, *Show Us How You Do It*, 137.

Transformational Style

Scholars today would likely refer to the leadership practices of Larimore, Nichols, and Keeble as being *transformational* or *spiritual* as a spiritual leader seeks to encourage spiritual transformation through participation and a developed relationship.[45]

Spiritual leaders are determined to instill confidence and provide vision.[46] For the transformational leader, *spirituality* is defined as the essence of who we are as individuals.[47] Endeavoring to lead in ways that will encourage their groups to become truer versions of their spiritual selves, the transformational leader who is personally focused on being transformed, is primarily concerned that those he leads will be spiritually transformed as well. The transformative leader is even willing to risk disapproval and rejection in the interest of such spiritual transformation.[48]

Spiritual (or transformational) leaders see the potential in the individual and thus their "vision" becomes a critical component of their leadership style. *Vision* is the power the leader has to see, imagine, and perceive the good that God can do in a person's life.[49] Spiritual leaders exercise their values and personal growth in order to lead others in a way

---

[45] Shepherd, *Church Growth*, 99

[46] Gilbert Fairholm, *Capturing the Heart of Leadership: Spirituality and Community in the New American Workplace* (Westport, CT: Greenwood Publishing Group, 2000), 113.

[47] Fairholm, *Capturing the Heart of Leadership*, 6, 74, 76, 77, 107, 112, 160.

[48] William H. Willimon, *Pastor: The Theology and Practice of Ordained Ministry* (Nashville, TN: Abingdon Press, 2016), 285.

[49] Robert D. Dale, *Pastoral Leadership* (Nashville, TN: Abingdon Press, 2001), 95.

that edifies them and enables them to achieve spiritual growth. By seeing their mentors lead from the standpoint of true, biblical, and spiritual values, those who are led recognize that their leaders are genuinely concerned with their eternal well-being as well as their happiness in life. Transformational leaders seek to serve their people through the "Golden Rule," hoping to help them to become leaders, and to find fulfillment in their respective works.[50]

Spiritual leaders are principle-centered, rather than profit-centered. Being principle-centered requires a set of core spiritual values. The core values serve to guide the leaders and those being led. The values frequently attributed to spiritual leaders are loyalty and conviction to the word of God, His kingdom, and His mission.[51] For the spiritual leader, his concern is for the group (the shared values and goals), rather than any personal goals or ambitions.[52] The dream and vision of the spiritual leader, when mixed with the hopes of the mentee, will often emerge as shared goals.[53] By embracing shared values and working toward common goals, spiritual maturity and transformation can be achieved.

Conclusion

Effective ministerial training includes more than the mere transfer of information. Comprehensive orientation and training for mentors should be considered.[54] The mentoring

---

[50] Fairholm, *Capturing the Heart of Leadership*, 91.
[51] Shepherd, *Church* Growth, 102.
[52] Fairholm, *Capturing the Heart of Leadership*, 114.
[53] Dale, *To Dream Again, Again*, 64.
[54] Kretzschmar, "The Role of Relationship," 8.

practice is most effective when it is conscious and systematic.[55] Relationships are developed as teachers serve as mentors early in the educational experience, deliberately get involved with their students as individuals, and find ways to strengthen their faith and development beyond the classroom.

---

[55] Kretzschmar, 8.

Chapter Three

The Shepherd Leadership Model

The spiritual or transformational model is more closely related to the biblical model of *shepherd* leadership than any other model that has been reviewed. Within the other models of leadership, the practical stratagem of leadership is of utmost importance. With the shepherd leadership model, the leader is motivated primarily by his concern for those "sheep" which are entrusted to his care.[1] Thus, the transparent and genuine affection exhibited for the Lord's people by the leader provides a truer indication of a shepherd leader than the ministry techniques utilized.[2]

God's Leadership in the Old Testament

In the Old Testament, the verb of "shepherd" (*raah*) is translated to pasture, tend, feed, lead, and keep the flock.[3] The verb can also represent the entire job of a shepherd. A "shepherd" is simply a feeder or tender of sheep.[4] In the New Testament, the verbs *bosko* and *poimaino* are translated to

---

[1] Nathan H. Gunter, "For the Flock: Impetus for Shepherd Leadership in John 10," *The Journal of Applied Christian Leadership* 10, no. 1 (Spring 2016): 8–18.

[2] Gunter, "For the Flock," 10.

[3] William L. Holliday, *A Concise Hebrew and Aramaic Lexicon of the Old Testament* (Grand Rapids, MI: Eerdmans Publishing Company, 1988), 342. Francis Brown, S.R. Driver, Charles A. Briggs, and Wilhelm Gensenius, *The New Brown, Driver, Briggs, Gensenius Hebrew and English Lexicon* (Lafayette, IN: Associated Publishers and Authors, 1978), 944.

[4] William Wilson, *Wilson's Old Testament Word Studies* (Peabody, MA: Hendrickson, 1993), 388.

feed, herd, and tend as a shepherd.[5] Again, the entirety of the work can be represented in this word. Accordingly, in the New Testament a "shepherd" (*poimen*) is also one who herds or tends sheep.[6] For the purpose of this study, the shepherd metaphor[7] used throughout both testaments will be of primary importance.[8]

Shepherds were providers, guides, protectors, and constant companions of sheep. Sheep were totally dependent on shepherds for protection, rescuing, grazing, watering, shelter, and tending to injuries. Without a caring shepherd, sheep would not have lived long in the ancient world.[9] Using the shepherd as a metaphor, the shepherd leader concept in the Old Testament begins with God. He is depicted as a Shepherd to Israel (Gen. 48:15; Gen. 49:24).[10] Throughout the Old Testament, God is shown leading His flock (Ps. 31:3). He

---

[5] Walter Bauer, *A Greek English Lexicon of the New Testament and Other Early Christian Literature*, edited by Fredrick William Danker, third edition (Chicago: Chicago University Press, 2000), 842.

[6] Bauer, *A Greek English Lexicon of the New Testament*, 843.

[7] When used metaphorically in the Old Testament, shepherding signifies "ruling and teaching" people. See Brown, et. al., *The New Brown, Driver, Briggs, Gensenius Hebrew and English Lexicon*, 944–5.

[8] The comparative nature of human leadership and shepherding will be the basis for the following study. Laniak notes, "Shepherd is a felicitous metaphor for human leadership because both occupations have a comparable variety of diverse tasks that are constantly negotiated." Timothy S. Laniak, *Shepherds after My Own Heart: Pastoral Traditions and Leadership in the Bible* (Downers Grove, IL: Inter-Varsity Press, 2006), 40.

[9] Leland Ryken, James C. Wilhoit, Tremper Longman III, "Sheep, Shepherd" in *Dictionary of Biblical Imagery* (Downers Grove, IL Inter-Varsity Press, 1998), 782.

[10] For more Old Testament depictions of God acting as a shepherd, see Ps. 79:13; Ps. 80:1; Ps. 95:7; Ps. 100:3; Isa. 63:11; Mic. 7:14; Zech. 9:16.

leads out of love (Exod. 15:13)[11] and goes before them (Ps. 68:7), driving out the enemy to make room for His own flock (Ps. 78:52–55). The Shepherd Psalm (Ps. 23) depicts God as a personal Shepherd (v.1) who leads His sheep to pastures and waters (v.2), while protecting them with His rod and staff (v.4), even restoring them to health (v.3). He also gathers His sheep (Isa. 56:8) and carries them in His bosom to safety (Isa. 40:11; cf. Ps. 28:9). As Shepherd, God is presented guiding (Deut. 26:5–8; Ps. 77:20; 80:1), protecting (Ps. 78:52), saving (Ezek. 34:22), leading (Jer. 50:19; Mic. 2:12, 13), and keeping careful watch over His flock (Jer. 31:10; Ps. 121:4).

During Israel's Old Testament history, God did not merely serve as a Shepherd who led by example. To the contrary, He actively directed His flock in paths of righteousness (Ps. 23:3). God served as leader, protector, and ruler for Israel.[12] God led according to His core "values" of righteousness, holiness, justice, and love. God's reputation among the nations depended upon the standards of the people who bore His

---

[11] On one occasion God is viewed as shepherding with anger (Ps. 74:1).

[12] In many ancient kingdoms the shepherd metaphor also symbolized a ruler's relationship with his people. Rulers were described as demonstrating their legitimacy to rule by their ability to "pasture" their people. Hammurabi and many other rulers of ancient western Asia are called "shepherd" or described as "pasturing" their subjects. Cyrus of Persia is also depicted as God's shepherd who would drive the flock from their homeland (Isa. 44:28–45:1; cf. Jer. 23:8). This metaphor is also used with regard to armies and their commanders (1 Kings 22:17; Jer. 6:3). However, no ruling king in Israel or Judah is known to have directly borne this title. For information pertaining to the use of the shepherd metaphor in antiquity, see R. Laird Harris, Gleason L. Archer, Jr., and Bruce K. Waltke, *Theological Wordbook of the Old Testament* (Chicago: Moody Publishers, 1980), 853; Timothy S. Laniak, *Shepherds after My Own Heart*, 58–74; Gerhard Kittel, ed., *Theological Dictionary of the New Testament*, trans. Geoffrey W. Bromiley (Grand Rapids, MI: Eerdmans, 1984), 6: 487–8.

name.[13] He sought to remove wicked influences from the flock He pastured (Zech.10:3; 11:7). The goal, vision, and work of the flock were derived from His leadership, while being executed through their participation in His plan. God sought to encourage the spiritual transformation of His people through their participation and the mutual relationship developed through experienced faith and reward.[14]

God began the practice of utilizing "under shepherds"[15] to look after the needs of His vulnerable flock (cf. 2 Sam. 23:3–4).[16] Laniak described the under-shepherd as being the human instrument by which God comprehensively shepherded His flock.[17] Moses and Aaron are depicted as shepherds over the flock (Ps. 77:20; Isa. 63:11). God did not want Israel to be as sheep without a shepherd upon their deaths, and thus He appointed Joshua to shepherd leadership (Num. 27:16–21). The judges followed in this capacity (2 Sam. 7:7). David then

---

[13] Laniak, *Shepherds after My Own Heart*, 111.

[14] "The acknowledgement that Yahweh was the true shepherd of Israel grew out of the living religious experience of the people and is thus to be distinguished from the cold courtly style of the ANE. In invocation, in praise, in prayer for forgiveness, but also in temptation and despair, the worshipers know that they are still safe in the care of God the faithful shepherd." Moises Silva, ed., *The New International Dictionary of New Testament Theology and Exegesis*, rev. ed. (Grand Rapids, MI: Zondervan, 2014), 4:82–3.

[15] Laniak, *Shepherds*, 53.

[16] Laniak, 40.

[17] Laniak, 91.

served God and His flock as a shepherd king (2 Sam. 5:2; 1 Chron. 11:2; Ps. 78:70–72).[18]

God's desire was to give His flock shepherds after His own heart to feed them with knowledge and understanding (Jer. 3:15). Yet, contrasted against the faithful "under shepherds" provided by God were unfaithful leaders (shepherds) who transgressed the law of God (Jer. 2:8), and influenced the people to do likewise (Jer. 10:21; 12:10; 22:22; 23:1–2; 25:34–38; 50:6–7). The most infamous recounting of their wicked rule over God's flock is found in Ezekiel 34:1–10. Concerning the significance of this passage, Taylor observes,

> The word "shepherd" suggests leadership and caring, and it was therefore an appropriate metaphor to use for hereditary monarchs who might otherwise think only in terms of lording it over their people. Israelite history shows how rarely this ideal of responsible leadership was achieved, and Ezekiel was particularly conscious of the failures of the most recent kings before the exile (cf. 19:1–14; 21:25).[19]

One of the reasons why God needed Ezekiel to serve as a watchman for His people was because the men who were supposed to be doing that job were negligent. The Lord addressed this issue by asking, "Should not shepherds feed the flock?" (Ezekiel 34:2). Figuratively speaking, it was not

---

[18] Although David is designated a shepherd by God, no ruling king in Israel or Judah is known to have officially borne this title from the people. Gerhard Kittel, *Theological Dictionary of the New Testament*, 487–8.

[19] John B. Taylor, *Ezekiel: An Introduction and Commentary* (TOTC; Downers Grove, IL: Inter-Varsity Press, 1969), 219.

because there was a shortage of food that the flock was not being fed. The shepherds of the flock were fat and clothed (v.3) and were feeding themselves (v.10).[20] The rulers were not true spiritual leaders of the flock. As a result, the flock was scattered as sheep without a shepherd (v. 5; cf. Zech. 10:2). The rulers behaved like owners rather than hired servants.[21] They became hirelings and thieves.[22] The shepherds of Israel were not concerned with strengthening the weak, ministering to the sick and broken, bringing back those who had been driven away, or seeking the lost (Ezek. 34:3–4). Instead of functioning as godly and faithful keepers of the flock, they drove away the flock by ruling them with force and harshness (Ezek. 34:4).

The health and multiplication of a community was a sign of good leadership.[23] The condition and growth of a flock depends greatly on the care, attentiveness, and skill of the shepherd.[24] Responsible shepherds should know every member of their flock in terms of their birth circumstances, history of health, eating habits, and other idiosyncrasies.[25] Yet, the result of this failed leadership was a people "scattered because there was no shepherd" (Ezek. 34:5). The Lord said, "My sheep were scattered over the whole face of

---

[20] Daniel Block makes a strong case that the shepherds in this passage refer to the entire ruling class who are guilty of abusing their power, even gross malpractice, within the flock. For further reading see Daniel I. Block, *The Book of Ezekiel: Chapters 25–48* (NICOT; Grand Rapids, MI: Eerdmans Publishing Company, 1998), 282–3.
[21] Laniak, *Shepherds*, 34.
[22] Laniak, 38.
[23] Laniak, 51.
[24] Laniak, 53.
[25] Laniak, 57.

the earth, with no one to seek or search for them" (Ezek. 34:6). The shepherds of His people were negligent, irresponsible, and careless with the sacred work they had in overseeing God's flock. God unequivocally states: "I am against the shepherds" (Ezek. 34:10). Due to the negligence of the false shepherds of Israel, God would take the matter into His hands to seek and save the lost (Ezek. 34:11), to feed, water, and rest His flock (Ezek. 34:13 ff.), to bind the injured and strengthen the weak, and to destroy the wicked shepherds (Ezek. 34:16; cf. Zech. 11:7).[26]

The Old Testament prophets look ahead to a time when God would rescue His flock from the nations to which they were scattered (Ezek. 34:11 ff.), returning them to their homeland from captivity (Isa. 11:11; Jer. 23:3; Mic. 5:3; Zech. 10:3 ff.). Israel was in need of spiritual transformation and God would pour out upon them the "Spirit of grace and supplication" (Zech. 12:10) corresponding to a fountain being opened for sin and impurity (Zech. 13:1).[27] Israel was in need of greater understanding and assurance of God's capacity for

---

[26] In his classic work, E.W. Hengstenberg believed the two staffs of Zech. 11:7, called "Favor" and "Union" by the Lord, signify the two-fold danger of outward enemies and internal strife which was facing the flock. The staff of "Favor" represents the mercy of the Lord in securing the people from outward enemies, while the staff of "Union" denotes brotherly concord among the people. Thus, God's work as a faithful shepherd would involve settling strife among the flock as well. For further reading see E.W. Hengstenberg, *Christology of the Old Testament* (Grand Rapids, MI: Kregel Publications, 1970), 354.

[27] Richard Alan Fuhr, Jr., and Gary E. Yates, *The Message of the Twelve* (Nashville, TN: B&H Academic, 2016), 292.

forgiveness, to which the prophets speak with unanimity (Isa. 55:6–9; Jer. 31:34; Ezek. 36:25; 37:23).[28]

The Lord promised to establish one Shepherd over Israel (Mic. 5:4; Zech. 11:16).[29] The Shepherd would be from the line of David (Isa. 11:1 ff.; Jer. 23:5; Ezek. 34:23; Ezek. 37:24; Zech. 12:1–13:1). While being the Lord's Servant (Ezek. 34:23), the Shepherd would also be "prince among them" (Ezek. 34:24). Israel would be one nation again, with one king (Jer. 23:5; Ezek. 37:22–24). The "Ruler" would be born in Bethlehem, although He has existed from eternity (Mic. 5:2).[30] The Spirit of the Lord would be upon Him and He would Shepherd with wisdom and understanding, counsel and strength, knowledge and the fear of the Lord, while judging in righteousness (Isa. 11:1–5; cf. Ezek. 34:17). The Shepherd Servant would establish a new covenant between God and Israel, ensuring the ultimate forgiveness of sin (Jer. 31:31-34; Ezek. 34:25; Ezek. 37:26) and establishing peace between God and man (Mic. 5:5; Isa. 9:6 ff.). The Shepherd would eventually become King over all the earth (Zech. 14:9), after

---

[28] Christopher J.H. Wright, *Knowing Jesus through the Old Testament* (Downers Grove, IL: IVP Academic, 2014), 103.

[29] It is also foretold that God would raise "shepherds" (Jer. 23:4). Hengstenberg here argued against too much stress being given to the plural, believing every plural can be employed to designate a generic idea in Jeremiah. The generic idea was to be described in the individual of v.5. See Hengstenberg, *Christology in the Old Testament*, 658.

[30] It is becoming increasingly common for scholars to question who Micah is referring to in this passage. However, by the time of the New Testament, it was understood that this passage referred to the Messiah (see Matt. 2:4–6; cf. Luke 2:4). For an example of the questions abounding on this passage see Stephen G. Dempster, *Dominion and Dynasty: A Theology of the Hebrew Bible* (Downers Grove, IL: IVP Apollos, 2003), 185.

first being stricken by the people (Zech. 13:7), and for the people (Isa. 53:4 ff.).

The Good Shepherd

The writers of the New Testament make clear that the Shepherd to whom the prophets pointed was Jesus Christ. Not only does Jesus check all the boxes pertaining to the fulfillment of these prophecies,[31] He also exhibits the most admirable traits of a shepherd leader in the image of the Father (see Heb. 1:3). Jesus was a constant companion to the flock, especially the twelve disciples.[32] He sought to find the lost sheep that had been scattered (Matt. 10:6; Matt. 15:24; Luke 19:10; cf. Jer. 23:4, 5; Ezek. 34:5; Zech. 10:2 ff.). He was a shepherd to sheep who had none (Matt. 2:6; Mark 6:34). He shepherded out of compassion (Matt. 9:36; Mark 6:34; cf. Exod. 15:13). He was a friend to His flock (John 15:13–15), which consisted also of publicans and sinners (Matt. 11:19). His goal as Shepherd is to lead the flock to springs of the water of life where God will wipe every tear from their eyes (Rev. 7:7). To accomplish His purpose, Christ realized He would have to be stricken (cf. Zech. 13:7; Isa. 53:5, 8) and lay down His life for His sheep (John 10:17), that they might live (John 10:27–28).

Jesus Christ is the "good" Shepherd (John 10:11) and the great Shepherd of the sheep (Heb. 13:20). Of the passages in

---

[31] For further reading about the fulfillment of Messianic prophecies see J. Barton Payne, *Encyclopedia of Biblical Prophecy* (New York: Harper and Row, 1973), 645–50.

[32] So much was Jesus the constant companion to His flock that Matthew gives special notice of when He was not among them (cf. Matt. 14:13, 23).

the New Testament provided to confirm the fulfillment of Messianic prophecies, it would be difficult to find one which does more to fix an application of the "shepherd" prophecies and a metaphor of the Old Testament than does the tenth chapter of John's Gospel (vv.1-38).[33] The text presents the familiar concept of false shepherds similar to those condemned in the prophets. During the ministry of Christ, the Jewish religious leaders had come to rival the wicked shepherds of the time of the prophets.[34] The Good Shepherd who is Christ, in comparison with the Shepherd Father of the Old Testament, is the rightful leader of the scattered flock (cf. Matt. 2:6; 9:36; 10:6; 15:24; Mark 6:34). Jesus has the familiar voice the sheep recognize and follow (John 10:3-5, 16, 27). He leads them out and goes before them just as the Father has done for Israel (Ps.23:3; Ps. 31:3; Ps. 68:7). Jesus is contrasted against the wicked shepherds considered to be thieves and robbers (John 10:8). As the thief who comes to kill, to steal, and to destroy (John 10:10), Jesus has come to save, to rescue, and to give life (John 10:7, 9, 10). Unlike the false shepherds, who as mere hired hands abandon the flock and flee at the sight of danger (John10:12–13; cf. Ezek. 34:1–10), Jesus is willing to die (to lay down His life) to protect and save

---

[33] In recognition of this correlation, Klink relates this passage to Ps. 23, musing, "Because Christ is my shepherd, I shall not want." He sees this to be the main idea of the passage. For further reading see, Edward W. Klink III, *John* (ZECNT; Grand Rapids, MI: Zondervan, 2016), 455.

[34] G.K. Beale and D.A. Carson, *Commentary on the New Testament Use of the Old Testament* (Grand Rapids, MI: Baker Academic, 2007), 461–2.

His flock (John 10:11–15; cf. Zech. 13:7; Matt. 26:31–32; Mark 14:27–28).[35]

Jesus is the Servant Shepherd through whom God would lead His people and do His will (John 10:14–15, 18, 38; cf. Ezek. 34:11 ff.). He is the Shepherd which will gather all the sheep into one sheepfold (John 10:16; cf. Jer. 23:5; Ezek. 37:22–24). His protection is sure and strong. No one can snatch the sheep from the hand of the Good Shepherd (John10:28).[36] Thus, Jesus is depicted as a Shepherd to His flock, leading His flock, going before them, and protecting them. The relationship Jesus has with His disciples is central to His leadership effectiveness as the Good Shepherd. The imagery emphasizes the care and compassion of the Shepherd and the dependence of the flock upon Him.[37] The sheep know Him (cf. Amos 3:1–2), recognize and hear His voice, and faithfully follow Him.[38]

---

[35] J. Ramsey Michaels, *The Gospel of John* (NICNT; Grand Rapids, MI: Eerdmans Publishing Company, 2010), 586.

[36] Carson agrees that the focus of the power in this statement is on Christ's power to protect His sheep. For further reading see D.A. Carson, *The Gospel According to John* (PNTC; Grand Rapids, MI: Eerdmans Publishing Company, 1991), 392.

[37] Leland Ryken, et. al., "Sheep, Shepherd" in *Dictionary of Biblical Imagery*, 785.

[38] George R. Beasley-Murray explains the concept of an intimate relationship denoted in this passage, in particular in vv.14–15. "In vv 14–15 we have a good example of how concepts in different languages can draw close, yet still require discrimination. In the Greek tradition knowledge is thought of as analogous to *seeing*, with a view to grasping the nature of an object; for the Hebrew, knowledge means *experiencing* something. In the area of religion, therefore, knowledge of God for the Greek is primarily contemplation of the divine reality; for the Hebrew it means entering into a relationship with God. This latter is vividly, if not shatteringly, illustrated in Amos 3:1–2. On this background vv. 14–15 have a clear meaning: the mutual knowledge of the

Under-Shepherds

Pursuant to the shepherd imagery of Christ over the flock is the imagery of under-shepherds to follow His example in caring for the church. Just as the Father did not want Israel to be left as sheep without a shepherd upon the death of Moses (Num. 27:17), Christ did not want the church to be left without pastoral care upon His ascension to His throne in heaven (Acts 20:28-29; cf. Jer. 23:4).

It is in the utilization of under-shepherds that we find a combination of elements of strong, directive leadership, elements of collaboration, elements of participation, and elements of apprenticeship leading to the spiritual transformation of the disciples.[39] In truth, it appears that modern church leadership theories have been comprised of certain elements of the biblical shepherd model, while discarding other key elements. Only when all the principles set forth in the New Testament are included can the complete picture of shepherd leadership be viewed.

Shepherd and his "sheep" denotes an intimate relationship which reflects the fellowship of love between the Father and the Son. (In 17:21 it not only *reflects* but is *rooted* in that relationship, expressed in terms of the Son being 'in' the Father and the believers being 'in' the Son." George R. Beasley-Murray, *John* (WBC; Nashville, TN: Thomas Nelson Publishers, 1999), 170.

[39] Walton has keenly observed one modern practice exempted from the shepherd leader model. He writes, "Political wrangling does not take place in Yahweh's council, and his rule is supreme." John H. Walton, *Old Testament Theology for Christians: From Ancient Context to Enduring Belief* (Downers Grove, IL: IVP Academic, 2017), 41.

As an under-shepherd, Peter was entrusted with the responsibility to feed the sheep (John 21:15-17).[40] Peter's work of feeding centered upon teaching and preaching, or "the ministry of the word" (Acts 6:4). While tasked with feeding the flock, and granted a measure of authority, the apostles continued to view Christ as the Chief Shepherd and supreme Overseer of the church (1 Pet. 2:25; 1 Pet. 5:4; Heb. 13:20). The apostles recognized that the Lord added to the flock the souls who were being saved (Acts 2:42, 47; Col. 1:13). Moreover, the Lord called and sent the preachers (Rom. 10:14-17) who were commissioned with preaching the gospel, whereby calling others to Christ (2 Thess. 2:14). The apostles recognized that their work was to serve as humble stewards of the flock and of the work entrusted to their care (1 Pet. 4:10-11; 1 Cor. 4:1, 6). Sometimes the apostles were even required to shepherd one another, as was the case with Paul and Peter regarding fellowship between Jewish and Gentile brethren (Gal. 2:11-14) and as is the case in congregations which have accusations brought against an elder (1 Tim. 5:19-20).

Just as Jesus received the work of shepherding from His Father, He handed over the task to Peter and the rest of the apostles. Peter then passed along the function of shepherd leader to elders in the churches.[41] To ensure faithful nurturing, guidance, and protection for the flock, the Lord

---

[40] The New Testament passages noted must be considered against the backdrop of the wicked shepherds during the time of the Old Testament prophets as well as during the time of the ministry of Christ.

[41] Gert Breed, "The *Diakonia* of the Elders according to 1 Peter," *Die Skriflig* 50, no. 3 (August 2016): 4.

gave qualifications and stipulations for shepherd leaders in every congregation (1 Tim. 3:1–7; Titus 1:5–9).[42] Just as Jesus was a constant companion to the twelve, elders are to remain among the flock (1 Thess. 5:12; 1 Pet. 5:2), caring for, encouraging, and guiding the church.[43] Yet, the shepherd's ongoing challenge was teaching the flock to obey the Lord's commands.[44] Breed observes, "If 1 Peter 5:1–4 is seen as a description of the service of the elder, it is firstly clear that it is rooted in the authority of Christ; secondly, the service or ministry of the elder is intended to assist believers to persevere amidst suffering and temptations."

A shepherd leader directs the flock and helps the flock to navigate a faithful course in the world, determining direction for the flock, while following the lead of the Good Shepherd.[45] As shepherd leaders follow the example of Christ,[46] the church follows them (1 Cor. 11:1; Heb. 13:7; 1 Pet. 5:3). But, just as Christ did not lead by example *only* (cf. John 14:15; John 15:10), elders are not to lead *only* by example. The flock is commanded to obey and submit to those who are watching

---

[42] The New Testament depicts *elders* (pl.) serving as shepherd leaders within each congregation. See Acts 11:30; 14:23; 15:2, 4, 6, 22, 23; 16:4; 20:17, 28–29; 21:18; Titus 1:5; Heb. 13:7, 17. Elders were also called bishops, presbyters, pastors, shepherds, and overseers depending upon the passage and the given translation of the Bible. For an orthodox discussion of the duties of elders from the perspective of a scholar among churches of Christ in America, see Ferguson, *The Church of Christ*, 318 ff.

[43] K. Thomas Resane, "Leadership in the Church: The Shepherd Model," *Hervormde Teologiese Studies* 70, no. 1 (May 2014): 1–6.

[44] Resane, 2.

[45] Resane, 4.

[46] For Gunter, shepherd leaders must not only follow the techniques used by Christ, but even more so, His motivation for shepherding. See Gunter, "For the Flock," 9.

over their souls (Heb. 13:17). The elders have been entrusted with "charge" over the flock (1 Thess. 5:12). If the shepherd leaders are faithful in communicating the word of God, the flock must obediently follow them as they follow Christ (cf. Phil. 4:9).

The shepherd leader is a servant leader who oversees the flock as a voluntary service to the flock (1 Pet. 5:2), hoping to protect the sheep from harm.[47] His interest is not in lording over the flock (1 Pet. 5:3), like the wicked shepherds from the prophets or from the ministry of Christ. He *serves* because it is his desire to serve and to teach those whom he leads to be servants as well. By serving the flock, the shepherd is imitating the shepherd leadership of Christ (cf. Mark 10:43-45). Shepherd leaders are active participants in the ministry, serving as pedagogical models of proper behavior and desires.[48] Such leaders are desirous to see their flock involved in the ministry and mission of Christ and to use their talents and abilities to fulfill their respective ministries and thereby bring glory to God.

The desire to see the spiritual maturity and health of the flock realized prompts the development of relationship, discipleship, and biblical education. Sheep become transformed as they come to mimic the faith of the shepherd.[49] Through ongoing discipleship and a constant state of spiritual mindedness, the sheep are transformed and

---

[47] Breed, "The *Diakonia* of the Elders according to 1 Peter," 7.

[48] Gregory E. Lamb, "Saint Peter as 'Sympresbyteros': Mimetic Desire, Discipleship, and Education," *Christian Education Journal* 15, no. 2 (2018): 203.

[49] Such is the premise for Lamb's article. Gregory E. Lamb, "Saint Peter" 189–207.

develop the mind of Christ. Shepherds must lead the flock to an environment conducive to encouragement and edification, both individually and collectively. In such an environment spiritual growth will be achieved and numerical growth will occur (Eph. 4:11). The flock will be safe and multiply.

From Father to Son, Son to apostles, apostles to elders, elders must also encourage shepherd leadership among the flock. There is a point to which every Christian is called to provide pastoral care to one another, which is borne out in the numerous "one another" passages of the New Testament.[50] The mutual edification of the body of Christ consists of love, encouragement, forgiveness, fellowship, teaching, and care. Each of these actions should be considered an aspect of healthy shepherd leadership. Various relationships within the flock will also require direction and guidance to come from one another (see Titus 2:1–8). Each Christian should desire to be a shepherd leader when the situation calls for it, looking unto the example of the elders of the congregation, and ultimately unto Christ as the "Chief Shepherd and Overseer of our souls."

In addition to presenting modern mentoring theories and results from recent research, this study also seeks to examine the biblical mentoring experience within the context of the Christian Scriptures (particularly the New Testament) as it

---

[50] "One Another" passages in the New Testament include: John 13:34, 35; 15:12, 17; Rom. 12:10; 12:16; 13:8; 14:19; 15:14; 16:16; 1 Cor. 16:20; 2 Cor. 13:12; Gal. 5:13; 6:2; Eph. 4:2; 4:25; 4:32; 5:21 Col. 3:9; 3:13; 3:16; 1 Thess. 3:12; 4:9; 4:18; James 4:11; 5:9; 5:16; 1 Pet. 1:22; 3:8, 9; 5:5; 5:14; 1 John 3:11, 23, 4:7, 11, 12; 2 John 5).

seeks to explore the mentoring methodology of a school of preaching. Does the New Testament direct us toward a model for leadership? We believe it does and we believe that model to be shepherd leadership. In the next section of the literature review, attention will be given to the mentoring experiences which occurred from the perspective of the shepherd leadership model in the New Testament. Specifically considered will be those mentoring experiences which developed among preachers.

Conclusion

The mentoring relationships of Jesus and Paul have been provided to bring to light the effectiveness of mentoring preachers within the shepherd leadership model. In every way, they chose to mentor by using the shepherd leadership model introduced by God in the Old Testament. Preachers were mentored according to common goals and shared values. Mentees were enabled, equipped, and entrusted to continue the evangelistic labors of their mentors.

Shepherd leaders are motivated primarily by their concern for those "sheep" which are entrusted to their care.[51] With a true shepherd leader serving as a mentor, the leader will seek to encourage spiritual transformation through participation and a developed relationship.[52] Endeavoring to lead in ways that their groups will become truer versions of their spiritual selves, the shepherd leader, who is also personally focused on

---

[51] Gunter, "For the Flock," 8–18.
[52] Shepherd, *Church Growth*, 99.

being transformed, will be primarily concerned that those he leads will be spiritually transformed as well.

Chapter Four

Mentoring Preachers in the New Testament

In recent years, a flurry of researchers sought to inform Christian universities, seminaries, and schools of the need to integrate Christian faith, principles, and virtues[1] by providing training supported by effective mentoring.[2] Biblical mentoring requires students to be mentored toward greater spiritual maturity and preparedness for ministry according to biblical leadership principles. Chiroma has said mentoring in the ministry context means

> to develop the potential capacity and competence of these individuals in the ministry as an accommodating learning relationship between a caring individual who shares knowledge, values, attitudes, experience and wisdom with another individual.[3]

Brueggemann considers the practice of mentoring to be as old as the social relationships in which knowledge is imparted from one to another in order to help that person flourish with well-being and success.[4] While certain aspects of mentoring could possibly be traced to the dawn of time, the study of the subject in the New Testament can become somewhat tricky,

---

[1] White, "Maintaining Christian Virtues and Ethos," 1.
[2] Chiroma, "Mentoring," 1.
[3] Chiroma, 2.
[4] Walter Brueggemann, "Mentoring in the Old Testament," in *Mentoring: Biblical, Theological, and Practical Perspectives*, ed. Dean K. Thompson and D. Cameron Murchison (Grand Rapids, MI: Eerdmans Publishing Company, 2018), 7.

as the equivalent to our English word *mentor* is not readily available in New Testament Greek.[5] While a clear equivalency in Koine Greek and modern English words might be lacking, all of the functions of the mentor can still be studied from the New Testament. One finds all the necessary components of a leader who is interested in the spiritual and transformational growth of the group when observing the shepherd leadership model. Moreover, in this model are found all the required functions for a spiritual mentor-mentee relationship.

In this section, the mentoring experiences of two preachers in the New Testament (Jesus and Paul) will be observed. Each of the mentoring experiences to be considered occurred within the shepherd leadership model. In the chart below are listed seven functions of the shepherd leader collected from previous sections of this study. A brief explanation has been included to illustrate the correlation between the shepherd leadership model and the biblical mentoring experience.

Function	Explanation
1. Exemplify	The shepherd leader follows and imitates God. As a mentor, he sets an example to the mentee of godliness, faithfulness, and servanthood.
2. Feed	The shepherd leader feeds the sheep. As a mentor, he provides teaching which will enable the mentee to obey God and to follow His word.

---

[5] David L. Bartlett, "Mentoring in the New Testament," in *Mentoring: Biblical, Theological, and Practical Perspectives*," 23.

3. Protect	The shepherd leader protects the sheep from harmful enemies and influences. As a mentor, he helps the mentee to recognize false teachers, false doctrines, and the threat of worldliness among God's people.
4. Fellowship	The shepherd leader is a companion to his flock. As a mentor a relationship through companionship is developed with the mentee. The relationship is built upon trust, shared values, and shared goals.[6]
5. Edify	The shepherd leader is keenly interested and actively involved in the growth and health of his sheep. As a mentor, he seeks the spiritual growth and maturity of the mentee. He encourages the mentee to learn, grow, and persevere, as well as to unlearn bad habits and retrain his thinking when necessary.[7]
6. Equip	The shepherd leader desires to equip his flock with the tools, mindset, and experience required to be faithful to God. As mentor, he recognizes the ability and encourages the utilization of the talents of

---

[6] Bartlett adds, "Insofar as this becomes a model for mentoring, the Christian mentor always relates to the other in hope." See Bartlett, "Mentoring in the New Testament," 31.

[7] For further discussion of "unlearning" bad practices in the ministry setting, see Thomas W. Currie, "Theological-Pastoral Perspectives on Mentoring," in *Mentoring: Biblical, Theological, and Practical Perspectives*, ed. Dean K. Thompson and D. Cameron Murchison (Grand Rapids, MI: Eerdmans Publishing Company, 2018), 47.

the mentee.

7. Entrust

The shepherd leader's goal is to see his flock actively and faithfully serving God and ministering to others in His kingdom. As a mentor, he entrusts the mentee with work to do. He provides an opportunity for the mentee to become an active participant and valued contributor in the ministry.

Jesus and the Twelve

In Christ is found an example of a preacher mentoring preachers through the shepherd leadership model.[8] Jesus mentored the twelve disciples as a group and each disciple as an individual.[9] Jesus loved them unto the end (John 13:1). He taught an object lesson by washing their feet (John 13:4–17), specifically instructing the twelve as to why this was necessary

---

[8] Bartlett asserts that "mentor" is not an adequate title for Jesus. See Bartlett, "Mentoring in the New Testament," 34. We agree that Jesus is much more than a mentor. Such also seems to be a moot point, however, as Jesus abhorred the use of religious titles altogether (Matt. 23:8, 9). The question before us is not whether Jesus should bear the title of "Mentor" but whether or not Jesus mentored the twelve. If so, can His practices be utilized by preachers mentoring preacher students today? Clinton recognizes, "Both Jesus and Paul used mentoring. They had individual relationships with trainees. But they also combined individual mentoring relationships with training of groups." He further states, "Mentoring will be one of the dominant forces in the training of emerging leaders in the years to come." See J. Robert Clinton, *Titus: Apostolic Leadership* (Altadena, CA: Barnabas Publishers, 2001), 159.

[9] It is important to note that Jesus mentored the twelve by using an informal apprenticeship style of mentoring. See Clinton, *Titus*, 157. The challenge for a school of preaching desiring to implement such a model would be to design a program which allowed for more time to be spent in such a capacity. Some formalities could be required from an organizational standpoint.

(vv.12–17). By being a friend to tax collectors and sinners, the Lord's actions proved to the twelve that every soul was valuable to God (Luke 7:34). He also exemplified obedience to the Father even unto His death on the cross (cf. Heb. 5:8, 9; 1 Pet. 2:21 ff.).

Jesus protected the twelve by warning them of the wolves in the world (Luke 10:3) and the leaven of the Pharisees' false righteousness (Luke 12:1). He promised to continue to protect them as they heard and followed Him (John 10:27, 28). Jesus fed the twelve through His sermons and personal teachings with a diet of sound doctrine intended to bring them to greater understanding of obedience and true holiness (cf. Matt. 5–7; Matt. 23). He oversaw the spiritual growth of the twelve by helping them to *learn* what was needed (e.g. Luke 11:1–4) and to *unlearn* when necessary (cf. Matt. 20:20–28).[10] Jesus provided opportunities for the twelve to work, to utilize their abilities and gifts, and to gain valuable experience (cf. Matt. 10). He was their constant companion and friend (John 15:13, 14).[11]

---

[10] Currie muses, "Unlearning seems to have constituted a good deal of Jesus' conversations with his disciples...Indeed, unlearning seems to describe the way Jesus mentors his disciples most of the time: 'You have heard it said of old...but I say unto you.' There is much to unlearn in being mentored as a theologian of this Lord." Thomas W. Currie, "Theological-Pastoral Perspectives on Mentoring," 47.

[11] Currie adds, "Theologians and pastors depend upon friends. Not all mentors are friends and certainly not all friends are mentors. But the best mentors in the field of study and teaching and ministry are often those friends and peers who share in the joys and burdens of this work and who are able to suggest, question, and even inspire their colleagues." Currie, "Theological-Pastoral Perspectives on Mentoring," 51.

He equipped His disciples for a greater purpose, teaching them the value of serving others as did He (Mark 10:44, 45). He entrusted them with the work of continuing His mission of seeking and saving the lost by preaching the gospel to the world (Matt. 28:19, 20; Mark 16:15, 16; Luke 24:47, 48; cf. Luke 19:10). In every way, Jesus was a mentor to the twelve. He chose to mentor by using the shepherd leadership model His Father introduced in the Old Testament. His relationship with the disciples was based upon His example, His feeding and nurturing, His protection, His fellowship, His edification, His equipping, and His entrusting. As mentees, the disciples had to receive the wisdom and guidance imparted by their Shepherd Mentor. Eleven of them chose to follow Him. One betrayed Him.[12]

Paul, Timothy, and Titus

Paul provides a second example of a preacher who mentored preachers through the shepherd leadership model. As with Christ, Paul's mentoring of others was informal, as fellow preachers worked alongside Paul as apprentices – at least for a while. Paul's relationship with Timothy serves as one example of his mentoring relationships. Timothy did not have a believing father, so Paul became a father figure in the faith to him (see 1 Tim. 1:2, 18; 2 Tim. 1:2; 2:1). From their

---

[12] The betrayal of Judas demonstrates two sides of the same coin. For the mentoring experience to be successful, the mentee must desire and follow the guidance of the mentor. Judas' betrayal teaches us that a person can literally have the Son of God as a mentor and still lack the necessary spiritual qualities to be successful in ministry. Failure to persevere in ministry is not always due to the fault, lack, or inferiority of mentors.

first encounter, Paul took Timothy unto himself as a mentee.[13] Timothy became a trusted companion to Paul in Asia, Macedonia, and Achaia (cf. Acts 18:5; 19:22; 20:4; Rom. 16:21; 2 Cor. 1:1; Phil. 1:1; Col. 1:1; 1 Thess. 1:1; 2 Thess. 1:1; Philem. 1). Paul equipped, nurtured, and encouraged Timothy until his death, and for ministry after his death (cf. 2 Tim. 4:1–8). He trusted Timothy in the work as his own son and fellow worker (Acts 17:14; 1 Cor. 4:17; 16:10; 2 Cor. 1:19; Phil. 2:19; 1 Thess. 3:2, 6).

The two letters written to Timothy by Paul are especially telling when considering Paul's role as a mentor to him.[14] Paul wrote to Timothy concerning conduct in the church (1 Tim. 3:15). Various matters of church polity were discussed (1 Tim. 2, 3, 5).[15] The letter contains instruction to protect Timothy from false doctrines and false teachers (1 Tim. 1:3, 4, 6; 2:18–20; 4:1–3). Encouragement is also given to take heed to his

---

[13] F.F. Bruce provides a good explanation as to why Paul had Timothy circumcised. Having a Jewish mother, Timothy was considered Jewish. But, having a Gentile father, Timothy was considered an apostate Jew. Timothy's apostate status would have jeopardized Paul's preaching in the synagogues of the area. F.F. Bruce, *The Book of Acts,* revised edition (NICNT; Grand Rapids, MI: Eerdmans Publishing Company, 1988), 304–5. We would add that his apostate status would have also prohibited Timothy's inclusion in that ministry setting.

[14] A few scholars over the past 200 years have questioned Pauline authorship of the Pastoral Epistles. This appears to be a recent development in biblical criticism as all three letters were widely accepted as authoritative and Pauline by the end of the second century. See William D. Mounce, *Pastoral Epistles* (WBC; Nashville, TN: Thomas Nelson Publishers, 2000), lxiv.

[15] Paul was depending upon Timothy and Titus to build upon the work previously done in the churches. The work was being entrusted to them to continue faithfully with evangelistic zeal, determination, and a strong work ethic. For further discussion on "work ethic" in the Pastoral Epistles, see Robert W. Yarbrough, *The Letters to Timothy and Titus* (PNTC; Grand Rapids, MI: Eerdmans Publishing Company, 2018), 30–41.

ministry (1 Tim. 4:12–16) and to maintain a holy and faithful life until the appearing of Christ (1 Tim. 6:11–16).

In 2 Timothy, Paul encouraged Timothy to use his gifts (2 Tim. 1:6, 7). He was encouraged to hold fast to the pattern of sound words (2 Tim. 1:13). Timothy was instructed to mentor others as he had been mentored by Paul (2 Tim. 2:2, 3). He was told to continue studying and to continue refuting error (2 Tim. 2:15, 16). Timothy was reassured in the inspiration of the scriptures (2 Tim. 3:15–17) and charged to preach the scriptures faithfully (2 Tim. 4:1–4), looking to Paul as an example (vv.5–8). Their friendship becomes apparent once again as the letter closes with Paul's desire to see him soon (2 Tim. 4:9, 21).

In every way, Paul was a mentor to Timothy. He chose to mentor by using the shepherd leadership model exemplified by Christ. His relationship with Timothy was based upon a common goal and the shared values of preaching the gospel and saving the lost.[16] He could challenge Timothy to genuine and frank self-assessment.[17] As a mentee, Timothy was more like a son to Paul.[18] He became a trusted coworker and someone Paul could depend on to build upon his labors.[19]

Paul's relationship with Titus also serves as an example of a preacher mentoring another preacher informally as an apprentice. In the case of Paul and Titus, the age discrepancy

---

[16] Bartlett observes, "The relationship between the two is built upon imitation, exhortation, and hope." Bartlett, 32.

[17] See Yarbrough's comments on 2 Timothy 1:6–14. Robert W. Yarbrough, *The Letters to Timothy and Titus*, 354.

[18] See 1 Tim. 1:2, 18; 2 Tim. 1:2; 2:1.

[19] Yarbrough, *Timothy and Titus*, 5.

between the two may not have been as large as it was with Paul and Timothy.[20] No mention is ever made of his youth as it was with Timothy (1 Tim. 4:12). Certainly, Titus was not a novice.[21] However, like Timothy, he is regarded as a son in the faith by Paul (Titus 1:4).[22]

Titus traveled with Paul to Jerusalem to discuss the matter of Gentile circumcision (Gal. 2:1). Paul could trust Titus to walk in the same spirit (2 Cor. 12:18). He was trusted significantly in communicating with the churches of Macedonia and Achaia and handling the delicate matter of their contribution to Judea (2 Cor. 7:13, 14; 8:6, 16, 23). During such times as he was absent from Paul, the apostle sincerely worried about Titus' wellbeing (2 Cor. 2:13; 7:6). In the epistle to Titus, Titus is trusted with appointing elders in Crete (Titus 1:5–9). He is warned about false teachers and emboldened to confront them (Titus 1:11–16). Titus is instructed to see to the mentoring practices among the Christians he serves (Titus 2:1–8). He is encouraged to speak the grace of God and the mission of Christ boldly and with all authority (Titus 2:11–15). The third chapter of the letter contains practical advice for ministry (Titus 3:1–11). What should Titus emphasize in his teaching? What type of teaching and individual should be avoided? Paul is also anxious to see

---

[20] The ages of Titus and Timothy are significant to this study as in schools of preaching ages vary as well. Some students enroll directly from high school. Some students wait a while to enroll and are older and more mature.

[21] Yarbrough, *Timothy and Titus*, 52.

[22] It is important to note that Paul did not have children. Timothy and Titus were his "sons" whom he loved dearly.

Titus as his love for his mentee is evident to all (Titus 3:12–15).

As Paul was a mentor to Timothy, he also mentored Titus. He chose to mentor by using the shepherd leadership model exemplified by Christ. His relationship with Titus was based upon a common goal and the shared values of preaching the gospel, edifying the church, and saving the lost. Titus became a trusted coworker and someone Paul could depend upon to continue his ministry.[23]

Conclusion

Having studied the mentoring experiences of preachers in the New Testament and the dynamics of the shepherd leadership model for the biblical mentoring experience, our attention will now center upon the mentoring practices of the preachers and students in a school of preaching. Can these biblical experiences be replicated within the context of a school of preaching? Are the mentoring experiences of schools of preaching patterned after the mentoring experiences of the New Testament? Can the mentoring

---

[23] Currie beautifully discusses this aspect of the preacher-mentor and preacher-mentee relationship. He writes, "That is why mentoring and apprenticeship in the field of theology and pastoral ministry can never be boring or tedious chores. Working together toward a common vision of great hope and beauty; learning to follow, to listen, to read carefully both text and person; learning to unlearn one's own certainties in the course of ministering to those whom God has given us to love; being mentored by peers and friends who accompany us on our way; discovering the fierce passion of God's love for this world and the costly and surprisingly liberating work that marks our participation in that love – these are the ways mentoring and apprenticeship in theology and pastoral ministry are made possible and become occasions for joy. See Currie, "Theological-Pastoral Perspectives on Mentoring," 53.

experiences of schools of preaching be patterned after the mentoring experiences of the New Testament?

Chapter Five

Mentoring in a School of Preaching
A Case Study

Seeking to discover and understand the mentoring practices as experienced by ministry students within a school of preaching operated by churches of Christ, graduates from a purposefully chosen school of preaching served as the populace for this research. Data was collected from in-depth individual interviews, consisting of open-ended questions and Likert scales, with graduates who agreed to participate. The interview questions focused on the types of mentoring experiences the graduates had and the comparison of those experiences to the biblical shepherd model of spiritual leadership and modern mentoring theory.

The method for developing a code structure in this research was purely inductive and grounded. Every line of each transcript was coded *de novo* (line by line). The coding required constant comparisons as new data was acquired and new themes emerged. The researcher chose this method so that he might limit the possibility of forcing upon the project any preconceived results. The interview questions led to answering the following research questions:

(1) How did the mentoring experiences of the graduates of the selected school of preaching affect their learning and preparation for ministry while in the respective program?

(2) How did these mentorship experiences affect the graduates and their respective ministries post-graduation?

(3) Did the graduates experience a mentoring relationship that was in harmony with the biblical shepherding model of spiritual leadership?

Before proceeding to questions pertaining to the actual mentoring experiences of the graduates during the interview, it was important for the researcher first to ascertain the participants' personal and unique understanding of the mentoring relationship. The first interview question sought to determine: What is your understanding of the responsibilities of the mentor and of the one being mentored in the mentoring relationship? The participants' answers to this question indicated an understanding of the mentoring relationship which corresponds to modern mentoring theory and the biblical model of shepherd leadership as explained in a previous chapter.

One participant acknowledged his personal understanding of the mentoring relationship by relating the need for accessibility on the part of the mentor, example-setting by the mentor, and a joint-partnership between the mentor and mentee. Generally, the graduates of this school of preaching believed the mentor should first and foremost be a teacher of the word of God. He should set an example of morals, ethics, and integrity. He should practice a high standard of Christian living. The mentor should be accessible. He should provide life lessons which correspond to his biblical teachings. He should provide moral and ethical support, encouragement, and tools to succeed in ministry. The mentor should have knowledge of ministry from prior experience and be willing to share those experiences with his students. The students looked to their mentors to prepare them for ministry by developing a relationship through which wisdom and knowledge for life in ministry could be imparted.

The participants also realized that effective mentoring involved mutual responsibilities of both the mentor and the mentee. The responsibilities of the mentee include sitting at the feet of the mentor, listening, and learning. The mentee should be expected to be humble and willing to take criticism, correction, and instruction. The mentee must be willing to do what is being taught by the mentor and make application of the instructions given. The mentee must be willing to discern whether that which is being taught is indeed the word of God. The mentee should also be willing to apply himself fully to the learning process, to take it seriously, and be to ask questions.

Having satisfied our concern that the participants understood the mentor-mentee relationship, we proceeded to developing an understanding of their mentoring experiences. Our research questions served to outline and guide our presentation, analysis, and interpretation of the data.

(1) **How did the mentoring experiences of the graduates of the selected school of preaching affect their learning and preparation for ministry while in the respective program?**

As we sought to answer this first question, we found that the impact of the mentoring relationships upon the students was extremely positive. One student spoke of how his relationship with his teachers caused him to enjoy going to class. The participants were mentored in a small group with relatively small class sizes (usually 1–10 students). They were inspired to become part of the legacy of the school and aspired to go about their work as students with a zeal which mirrored that of the teachers.

A Legacy

Through the mentoring experiences in school, the students began to appreciate a legacy which was theirs to continue. The idea of contributing to and maintaining a legacy was motivational to the students, as one participant expressed,

> It encouraged us to do the work better because we wanted to make them proud; but we also wanted to live up to their legacy. And that was a big deal at the school. The school of preaching was their legacy, and you could feel it. And that's why you wanted to have these mentors; because you wanted to sit at their feet and learn everything you could.

Another participant related that the legacy was equally important to the teachers. He said,

> They are encouraging you because you're the next generation coming up. They would often bring that up… We're going to be replacing them at some point in time. We need to hear…and to hold to the truth. I think that is very important. It made you want to do well for them.

Many of the participants noted that having good grades was not the most important aspect of their educational experience. They wanted to learn "information to pass on to the next generation, to your generation, to the generation that comes after you." One participant said the teachers stressed this "and encouraged that either in preaching or writing or debating.... that we need solid men to come forward from the next class to the next class." Concerning "passing the torch" from teacher to student, one participant added,

> That's exactly how I felt. Exactly how I felt. You know what? The knowledge and information that they had is incredible, so to sit at their feet, so to speak, for just that short period of time and gain some of what they know and some of what they have studied so hard to learn, it's a blessing. It was a blessing, and still is when I get a chance to talk to those folks.

The legacy being handed down to the students prompted the development of the mentoring relationship, discipleship, and biblical education. The concept of being part of a legacy motivated them to take ownership in the school and to maintain the work they were doing by taking their studies seriously. Through the shared legacy of the school, the students recognized they were part of something bigger than themselves and strove to make their unique contribution to the betterment of the learning environment they were provided.

The Sacrifices Made by the Teachers

Another unique theme from this study is the motivation students received for their studies when they saw the sacrifices their teachers were making to teach and mentor them. Many of the teachers were driving from 3 to 4 hours in distance to teach at the school. Most of the teachers were not fulltime faculty members, meaning they received only a small stipend for their work. While the distance they traveled had an adverse effect on the amount of time some teachers were able to spend with the students, the sacrifice they made to be teaching at the school did not go unnoticed. One student stated,

> I wanted to be pleasing to all the teachers, all the ones that taught me. I wanted to make sure that I was giving my very best effort because as I looked to them, I saw them giving their very best effort. I worked hard and I studied hard. I wanted to do well, but I didn't want to, by any means, be a disappointment to them…. I didn't want to be a disappointment for those that were working so hard to teach me and help me.

As the participants came to value the sacrifices of their teachers, their recognition of the need for selflessness and service in ministry increased. They were humbled by the sacrifices their teachers were willing to make for them. They came to appreciate the efforts being taken to ensure they were taught and prepared for ministry. Such recognition and appreciation, in turn, motivated greater effort and developed a greater understanding for learning in the scholastic environment of the school of preaching.

Time Management

The learning experience was also enhanced by an improvement in time management skills. One participant spoke of how a close relationship with a mentor caused him to evaluate his attitude toward his assignments, saying,

> I tended to let small assignments just kind of slip. In large part, particularly because of my relationship with one instructor, I had to take a long, hard look at how I was treating that opportunity for an education. I realized I wasn't hurting anybody but myself… I think it helped me kind of buckle down and really do the work. Because with any school of preaching, I think, you can skate by if you really want to, but you're going to get out of it what you put in it.

Concerning teachers' work ethic as witnessed by the students, another participant observed,

> I think what really comes through from those mentors is the work ethic that they put in to their ministry and on their own personal work and the diligence on their own personal study.

The work ethic of the teachers was a recurring statement from the participants. The graduates saw the time and effort put into their classes while also realizing these teachers were dedicated to fulltime ministry in churches of Christ. The participants saw the need for organization and structure in the lives of their mentors and came to understand that such organization and structure required a prudent use of time. If they were to stay on top of their studies and future requirements in ministry, they would have to stay organized, do their research, and keep up with their assignments. Not only were the students motivated to study, but their mentors taught them how to study. Of his learning experience, one graduate said, "I learned more about how to research effectively and timely." He continued, "I am not going to be someone who fails because I didn't put the effort into something."

The Bible was at the core of the school's curriculum. The school offered the students a rigorous two-year program in biblical and ministerial studies. One student referred to it as a "meat grinder." Another student called it a "24/7 Bible Boot Camp." Two participants said plainly it was not for new converts or for Christians uncertain about entering ministry. A few participants spoke about the intense study required for learning New Testament Greek. One frankly said he would not have been able to finish the Greek studies without the support of his mentors. Overall, the graduates appreciated the instructors' depth of biblical knowledge, their knowledge of biblical backgrounds, the ability afforded them to learn subjects which they had not previously studied, and the way the instructors explained their ideas. One participant related the uniqueness of the program by saying,

> It's not like a four-year program or even a master's degree or where you have maybe four to six years of study. You had two years to soak up as much information as you can learn, not just what the word of God says, but also to learn how to study and how to prepare for a life of study.

The influence his mentors had on this student was "phenomenal" and contributed significantly to his success as a student in this intense learning atmosphere as they helped him "learn how to study."

Realizing Potential and Ability

The participants frequently spoke of their mentors encouraging them to learn and grow to the best of their ability. One participant candidly related,

> There were some teachers that I wasn't as close to. There were some that I was convinced hated me. It turned out that they just saw a great deal of potential in me. And they really pushed me and really gave me a hard time in order to weed out some of the bad things from my personality and to help me strengthen some others.

Another graduate said,

> There's a genuine desire to see everybody succeed. And to me, that's really kind of pushed it over the edge. That's what made it so good. The relationship that you have, the teachers and you had with everybody on staff.

Through mentoring, a close relationship developed with the mentee. Another participant confessed, "I honestly don't believe that I could have done it any other way," as he considered the close relationships he had with the teachers and with the members of the congregation conducting the school. Another participant related his experience at the school during his first two weeks saying,

> I felt like, after the first few days, that I can't do this. Then the second week, I felt, it's hopeless. I'm a failure. I can't do this. I want to go home and quit.

A mentor encouraged him to not give up and to "stick it out." Of this mentor, the participant said,

> He was a great mentor and now he's someone that I greatly respect now and has encouraged me. He's someone that if I get married, Lord willing, would be the one that conducts the ceremony. He was always encouraging.

The mentoring experiences of a married student proved to be especially beneficial to him while advancing through the two-year program. He related,

> I think without the mentoring that I had, maybe I wouldn't have gotten quite as good a grade, especially if you know that it was hard being there as a family and not getting to hardly spend any time with my wife and children.

He concluded, "It was hard. It was hard on my family to be able to go to the school of preaching for two years."

The participants experienced a transparent and genuine affection from their mentors while in the school of preaching. It was expressed on multiple occasions how the school cared about their well-being, "not just their grades." The students in turn also seemed to place a greater emphasis on truly learning the Bible and being faithful to the word than on scoring highly on tests, papers, etc. The students wanted to score highly, but it does not appear that grades were more important than genuinely learning the text.

Summary

Just as Jesus equipped His disciples for a greater purpose, teaching them the value of serving others as did He (Mark 10:44, 45) and entrusting them with the work of continuing His mission of seeking and saving the lost by preaching the gospel to the world (Matt. 28:19, 20; Mark 16:15, 16; Luke 24:47, 48; cf. Luke 19:10), we have found that these students were equipped and inspired to continue the legacy of their mentors, i.e. the preaching of the gospel of Christ. Jesus chose to mentor by using the shepherd leadership model His Father introduced in the Old Testament. His relationship with the disciples was based upon His example, His feeding and nurturing, His protection, His fellowship, His edification, His equipping, and His entrusting. As mentees, the disciples had to receive the wisdom and guidance imparted by their Shepherd Mentor. The effect of the shepherd leadership model on the students in this school of preaching has been tremendous. The participants had shepherds who set before them an example of Christ-like service and sacrifice, nurtured, and fed them through their teaching, and equipped and entrusted them to continue in their work.

(2) How did these mentorship experiences affect the graduates and their respective ministries post-graduation?

The effect of mentoring on the ministry of these graduates after graduation is also one of the issues discovered in this study. We were interested to understand and explain the effects of the mentoring they received in school and the impact it had on their work as evangelists. We did not know what to expect, but soon became pleasantly informed about the effectiveness of the mentoring experiences of these graduates in their respective ministries in churches of Christ after graduation.

Avoiding Burnout

Our findings indicate an incredible rate of ministry retention among the graduates. Our study included the years 2010–2019. During these ten years, a total of 31 students graduated. We learned that 28 of the 31 are still active in ministry. Of the three graduates no longer active, we learned from the director of the school that one is unable to continue in ministry due to age and health limitations. No explanation was given for the other two. Without including the graduate who is no longer physically able to preach, the ministry retention rate is 93% for the decade. If he is included, the rate is still above 90%.

One participant said he was specifically mentored to take personal time for himself and his family. He was encouraged to pursue personal interests and hobbies to help him unwind from the stress of fulltime ministry. Another said he felt like they were being prepared for what fulltime ministry and service was like. The participants often remembered learning from the stories and experiences told by instructors in classes which provided real-world situations in ministry as a way of preparing them for the work. Upon entering ministry and reflecting on these experiences shared by his teachers, one participant came to believe "they were preparing us for what we would face."

Our research utilized Likert scales to assist in data analysis. We asked each participant: Using a scale of 1 to 10, (1 being very poor and 10 being ideal) how would you rate the effectiveness of your mentoring experiences upon your ministry post-graduation? The average answer was 8/10. We asked each participant: Has your satisfaction with ministry 1) increased; 2) decreased; or 3) remained constant over time? 60% of the participants said their satisfaction with ministry has increased. 33% said their satisfaction has remained the same. One of these said he "still loves it." 6% of the participants said their satisfaction with ministry has decreased, but only because they desire to be doing more than they are currently doing in ministry. 100% of the participants said they desire and are willing to mentor others if/when presented the opportunity.

Sermon/Class Preparation and Delivery

The extensive research done while in school has only enhanced the job efficacy of the participants pertaining to preaching and teaching. One graduate said,

> There's no sense wasting time doing it again. I can pull this research out that I've done, and I can apply it in other places, whether teaching a class or delivering a lecture.

Another graduate praised his mentors for giving him direction for future academic pursuits, ministry, and life. Many participants alluded to the tools they gained for ministry. Of these tools, most of the participants spoke of being taught how to reason and use logic in their studies. One said, "We were taught how to study." The participants seemed to appreciate how the curriculum of the school gave special attention to Christian evidences and apologetics. However, one criticism which recurred throughout the interviews was the lack of time and practical application for personal evangelism. Courses were taught, but little field work occurred. Evangelistic campaigns were recommended by a couple of participants as a solution to this perceived deficiency in the program. The participants who stated too little time was given to practical application and experience in the field of evangelism also believed too much time and emphasis was given to learning New Testament Greek. They indicated more balance was needed in these areas of study.

One participant expressed confidence that his mentors taught him how to preach "very sound biblical lessons." Concerning sermon preparation, homiletical fundamentals were hardly mentioned. Increased confidence and boldness when speaking was most often mentioned by the participants. The participants pointed to their increased knowledge and communication skills in correlation to their increased confidence in public speaking. Participants believed their style of preaching was enhanced, including their ability to communicate the message and persuade the listener. The increased ability to answer questions in Bible classes was also a contributing factor to their increased confidence.

People Skills and Conflict Management

A prominent theme which surfaced in our research was the encouragement and development of "people skills" for ministry. Participants continually alluded to training and lessons they received to help them address and handle controversial issues in ministry. They spoke of the patience which they witnessed in the demeanor of many of their mentors in school as being a contributing factor to helping them deal with possible conflicts in ministry. They credited their instructors with helping them in areas of conflict resolution and with developing the ability to listen to others and answer their questions respectfully. One participant recalled,

> There was one situation when I first started preaching at my first congregation after graduating that those sort of techniques that I learned on an individual basis, particularly about being able to analyze a situation and deal with people and that sort of thing. It allowed for a situation that could have divided the church to hold the church together. And we only lost one member actually at that point because they didn't agree with the decision that was made.

One graduate spoke specifically about the humility of a certain mentor in the school. He pointed to his example and people skills when dealing with elders in the church. This participant observed,

> He was a good example in his relationship with the elders as well. Even if, you know, he didn't perhaps agree with everything, or he might have wanted to do something different. He never said anything bad about the eldership and respected them and tried to pass that on to the students to respect their elders.

Summary

Our effort to answer this second research question has helped us to understand that the mentoring experiences of the participants while in the school of preaching carried over into real-world ministry experiences in the church. The graduates found they were better equipped to avoid burnout, to prepare and deliver sermons, to teach Bible classes, and to address and handle conflict and controversial issues in ministry.

(3) Did the graduates experience a mentoring relationship that was in harmony with the biblical shepherding model of spiritual leadership?

The first two research questions sought to discover the effectiveness of the mentoring experiences of the graduates pertaining to their time in school and their respective ministries. We have found that their mentoring experiences have been quite effective and positive for their studies and their ministries. With this third research question, we are seeking to know more about the mentoring that occurred and why it has been so effective.

We asked the participants: Would you say you experienced a mentoring experience that was in harmony with the biblical shepherding model of spiritual leadership? 100% of the participants said they believed that they received biblical shepherding from their mentors while in school. We also asked them: How many biblical mentors do you suppose you had in school? On average, the graduates gave the figure of 5.4%. We can safely conclude that each graduate on average had between 5–6 mentors who provided biblical shepherding to them while they were in the school. Participants were also asked to use a scale of 1 to 10, (1 being very poor and 10 being ideal) to quantify their satisfaction with the mentoring they received. The average answer was 8.9/10. When asked if their satisfaction with their mentoring experience has increased over time, 88.8% of the participants said it had increased.

When asked if the mentoring relationship had increased or decreased since graduation, 66.6% said the relationship had decreased. The participants acknowledged this was as much their responsibility as that of the mentor. They believed distance and the arrival of new students for teachers to mentor in the school were the most likely factors contributing to a decrease in the relationship. However, most participants attested to their continued love and appreciation for their mentors and their happiness to be with them when opportunities are presented. One participant even said, "Most of them are still mentors today. Even ten years removed from the school."

When asked to share their ideas for an ideal mentoring environment in a school of preaching setting, the following characteristics were presented: small class sizes; opportunities to develop relationships with the faculty, director, elders, and church members; having teachers who possess Christian character, have experience in ministry, and know what it takes to be successful in ministry; having teachers who understand each student is unique and will see their potential and push them to succeed; having teachers without an agenda, but are genuine; having a moral and spiritual environment at all times; having fulltime instructors on a regular basis so that relationships can be developed; having teachers who are father figures and are willing to take students under their wings; having a director who genuinely cares, who has an open-door policy, who they can trust, seek for comfort, and know will not be judgmental; having a faculty that is multi-talented with varying backgrounds of expertise; an atmosphere filled with people who genuinely desire to see the students succeed; an environment where fear of public speaking can be overcome and regular help in sermon delivery is offered; and one which provides opportunities to stay in contact with mentors after graduating from the school. With these characteristics in mind for an ideal mentoring environment in a school of preaching, we asked them to use a scale of 1 to 10, (1 being very poor and 10 being ideal) and to rate their mentoring experiences while in school. The average rating was 7.6/10. This number is lower than the overall satisfaction rating of 8.9/10. It shows that while the school may not have met every ideal characteristic, it still provided a satisfactory mentoring environment and beneficial experience for the students.

Informal Mentoring Model

Informal mentoring occurred more than formal mentoring in the school of preaching. Participants were asked: Would you describe the mentoring environment as being more formal and structured or informal and naturally experienced through relationships that developed over time? They stated that most of the mentoring occurred naturally during lunch breaks, in the library, and time spent outside of class. When given a scale to quantify the nature of the mentoring (1 being very unstructured and 10 being very structured), the average answer was 4.2/10. When asked how many hours were spent each week with mentors in an informal setting, the average answer was 6.8. One participant noted that the informal mentoring was "part of the culture of the school." To develop relationships and friendships with mentees outside of class, some teachers would even stay after school hours, making themselves accessible to the students. While class time was described as formal and structured, one participant described it as "all business," mentoring time was described as informal, organic, natural, and "very effective."

Participants believed the informal mentoring model helped to develop relationships as mentors and mentees grow closer; to create interest and to pay closer attention in class; and to learn how to behave as Christian men. On occasion, however, some students may have taken advantage of the relationship being developed. One participant remembered,

There were times when we students certainly abused it, especially coming back from lunch breaks at times. There was an instance where we showed up half an hour late from our lunch break and our teacher was teaching to an empty classroom. He was going through his lecture notes and everything. Just none of us were there. That's irresponsibility on the part of the students and taking advantage of the personal relationship rather than neglect on the part of the teacher.

While some students may have taken advantage of the relationships being developed with their mentors, it does not appear that the informal mentoring fostered a culture of favoritism or created an adverse effect on the professional relationship between teachers and students. A participant explained,

> There was always an understanding of that professional relationship. 'We are brothers in Christ. We are helping you learn,' but it never got too informal. I guess you'd say.

Another participant observed,

> In my opinion, I think it strengthened the relationship. It allowed us to feed off of their knowledge. We weren't afraid to approach them in that professional way. Yes, they are my professors and I need to ask them these things. I think at least for our class, we knew still there was a boundary where we could not take advantage. Yes, because we have a relationship and because we are brothers in Christ, I still had the papers, I needed to turn things in on time. There wasn't extra leeway because of that informal relationship and informal mentoring.

It was also recalled by another graduate who had a friendship with an instructor prior to enrolling in the school,

> You could definitely tell there is a difference between how they treat you in school than they do outside. I knew one of my one of my teachers since I was like five or six years old…They definitely didn't show favoritism. There's certainly a line that you knew not to cross. You're not going to get any favors or special charity just because you

knew them already. In fact, a really good friend of mine took me aside the first day we had classes and said, 'Look, I know we're really good friends, but there's a difference with me being a teacher.' It was very clear that they were there as teachers. There was a professionalism and they didn't treat me any different than they did the other people in my class, which I appreciated.

The school offered no formal mentoring sessions, programs, or activities, but this did not seem to deter mentoring from occurring. At this school of preaching, no comprehensive orientation and training for mentoring is offered to the teachers. Their effectiveness for mentoring has been developed through spiritual maturity, Bible knowledge, and their understanding and implementation of the biblical shepherd model of spiritual leadership. Even though no program of formal mentoring exists, the participants rated the environment 7.6/10; they rated the mentoring received 8.9/10; and the satisfaction with the mentoring they received has increased for 88.8% of them. Each participant had an average of 5 to 6 mentors as a student and spent an average of 6 to 7 hours per week with him in an informal setting.

The Teachers' Role as Shepherd Leaders

The graduates believed the responsibility of their teachers was to mentor them as much as it was to teach the assigned subject. They looked to their teachers as mentors and role models. The participants conveyed the belief that effective teaching in a school of preaching setting is enhanced when the teachers set a Christ-like example and have a high standard of Christian living, morals, ethics, and integrity. The participants spoke of the teachers' willingness to develop personal relationships with them, which increased their effectiveness as mentors. Spending time together and being accessible to the students were ideas repeated throughout the interview process. The participants of our study also looked to their teachers to impart "wisdom for life" and "life lessons" from their experiences in ministry. The participants wanted to gain knowledge for the work of God (what to expect in ministry) as much as they desired knowledge of the word of God. The participants in our study sought ethical and moral support from their teachers. They desired encouragement, forbearance, and at times forgiveness from them.

Equally important to the participants was the role of the mentee. They understood the mentee must be willing to "sit at the feet of the mentor," to pay attention, ask questions, listen, and learn. The mentee should be humble, willing to accept criticism, instruction, and correction. The participants understood that their mentoring experience was a "joint partnership" to be taken seriously, requiring both parties to apply themselves in the relationship.

The Director's Role as a Shepherd Leader

The school of preaching serving for this case study has had two directors during the specified time frame for our research (2010 – 2019). The first director of the school was regarded as a "key mentor" by one of participants. He served as an example of someone who possessed character; was supportive; was firm, but kind and loving; and remained involved in their lives after graduating from the school. Yet, he was also viewed as someone who tended to be more of an administrator and was not involved enough in the day-to-day mentoring of the students. When asked to rate him on a 1–10 scale (1 being very poor and 10 being ideal), his mentoring influence rated 7.5/10 by the participants.

The second director of the school considered in this case study was regarded as "a glue guy" for the school by one of the participants. The graduates considered him to be passionate; he helped them to realize their potential; he made himself available to the students; and he provided as much time as was necessary to mentor them. Several of the participants said he worked to develop personal relationships with them. One remembered fondly his encouragement to overcome a fear of public speaking.

However, some of the participants were concerned about his workload. He serves as the fulltime director for the school and is also a fulltime minister. It was said that he would help others to his own detriment and that he had "too much on his plate." One participant recalled:

> During my first year, I think he was as good a mentor as you could possibly ask for. He was available at all times, involved in the lives of the students, and really made an effort to get to know them, get to know us, get to know me. Between my first and second year, he transitioned from just being the director of the school of preaching to being the director and also the minister of the congregation…So he had to do two jobs, two full time jobs in the same amount of time…His focus shifted from the school of preaching to serving the congregation.

Understandably so. But, the ability to talk to him at that point became a little bit more difficult. He wasn't as available because he'd be out visiting, doing all kinds of things. And so the mentorship role in my second year that he had played in the first year really was drastically scaled back.

Another participant commented:

He is incredible at what he does. He is very clearly passionate about it. He is intelligent. The only thing I ever have a problem with is how much he stresses himself…I feel like he's overworked himself… And by the way, I am a little bit biased…besides my own father, he is the closest thing to a father I have.

One could sense the genuine love and concern the graduates have for this man, as one participant related:

And the director overseeing the program genuinely cared, not just about making sure that I went out and didn't preach anything that was false doctrine, but that I was getting an education, that I was growing and developing my faith and just concerned about my overall well-being. And to me, that makes a big difference. It's helped to build my trust in him to where I felt like I could come and ask him anything at any point in time. Fostering personal relationships is really what the school of preaching did for me.

Another participant spoke of the Christ-like example the director provided to him, as he offered the following statement:

I told people in the past that I don't know that I've ever seen anyone as Christ-like or gave me a better image of Christ as him. And part of that was that he was a director, but he directed it through his service. He wasn't the ruler with the iron fist guy or 'I'm the director of the school, so you have to listen to me.' It's very much, 'I'm going to serve you and to ask for you to humbly respect me.'

When asked to rate the second director on a scale of 1 – 10 (1 being very poor and 10 being ideal) for his contribution to their mentoring experiences in the school of preaching, the participants rated him 8.9/10.

The Elders' Role as Shepherd Leaders

The perception of the mentoring practices of the elders of the overseeing congregation of the school was split almost 50/50 between positive and negative feedback. On a scale of 1 – 10 (1 being very poor and 10 being ideal), the elders rated 4.9/10. Students who had a prior relationship with them rated them extremely high: 8.5/10. A couple of graduates who rated them poorly said that they were "detrimental" to the mentoring experience and "the most disappointing thing at the school was the lack of a relationship with the elders and the congregation." Usually, however, when the feedback was low, the participants cited that they did not have much of a relationship with them; the elders were busy doing other things, including working; their mentoring could be improved; and they left the mentoring to others. The most frequent comment was "they were hands off."

The elders of the congregation did not receive a low score necessarily because of a perceived lack of concern or positivity. While one graduate said they seemed "cold and distant," most of the participants viewed the elders as encouraging; providing good oversight; seeing to the needs of the students; being positive; providing opportunities for the students to serve in the worship services of the church; showing concern for them and their families; being willing to help; very good to answer questions; being good and capable men; and biblical elders. Here is one example of feedback received from the participants:

> The times I interacted with them were very positive. But it just wasn't that often…the most time I spent with the elders was when they were doing my interview for enrollment.
>
> I would see them. There was one elder that was there, most of them worked. There was one that would show up, one or two that would show up regularly for chapel. They were always encouraging.

Another participant believed,

> I think the biggest thing that they showed me is what an eldership ought to be like. I think that's what I learned from them. I think that they're very good and capable men and they might very well be the closest thing to a biblical eldership that I have had the privilege of seeing.

He went on to say he believed these men tried their best "to shepherd a flock conscientiously." He also said the elders were "very hands on when it comes to selecting students."

Another graduate added, "I would say they were they were very, very encouraging to the students and they continue to be. They were very welcoming." He told of the elders' concern for him as a student and as a father with a family. He added, "they were concerned about that and they expressed that over and over again...my experience was absolutely wonderful. I found them all to be just an incredible encouragement to me."

The Members' Role as Shepherd Leaders

A small group of the members of the hosting congregation did an effective job mentoring the participants while in the school. One participant gave an estimate of "ten" members who served as mentors. These would appear regularly for chapel service; offer encouragement; and take students under their wings. While the bulk of the congregation may not have been as involved, the participants generally felt "like we were part of the congregation" and that the church was "open and friendly to new students."

When asked to rate their mentoring experience as it related to the members of the hosting congregation from 1 – 10 (1 being very poor and 10 being ideal), the participants gave a rating of 6.8/10. One participant offered his insight, saying,

> I think they know exactly what their role is within the church. And I think they do it wonderfully. I don't think I ever had any bad run-ins with members of the congregation. The scale really wasn't that much from good

or bad. It was from good to apathetic. Which congregation can't say they had that?

When considering the influence of the members as mentors, another student added:

I probably shouldn't be, but it's fascinating to me to see their loving care for every student that comes there and their support shows with their language. There are several of them that are supportive monetarily...They come to chapel...I found them to be an unbelievable encouragement to all of us that were there. And we got to know them, several of the members on a personal basis...I found them to be some of the most positive, encouraging people in the world.

Summary

The mentoring model at the school of preaching was informal, greatly appreciated, and highly effective. On a 1 – 10 scale, the participants rated their mentoring according to the biblical shepherding model as an 8.9/10. The ratings descended from faculty (8.9), to directors (7.5 and 8.9), to members (6.8), to elders (4.9). The mentoring experiences of the participants in this case study had a tremendous impact on them while in the school of preaching and now that they are actively involved in ministry.

Conclusion

The problem addressed in this study is a lack of understanding for the mentoring practices as experienced within a school of preaching operated by churches of Christ. The research was conducted with the intention of explaining these mentoring practices by examining their methods and results. We sought to understand:

(1) How did the mentoring experiences of the graduates of the selected school of preaching affect their learning and preparation for ministry while in the respective program?

We have found that the legacy being handed down from the teachers to the students was a significant factor in prompting the development of the mentoring relationship. Discipleship, biblical education, and preparation for ministry resulted. The sacrificial examples of the teachers greatly influenced the students to work harder and to take their studies seriously. The mentors acted as shepherds, who set before the students an example of Christ-like service and sacrifice. As shepherd leaders, they nurtured and fed the students by teaching, equipping, and entrusting the students to continue in their work.

(2) How did these mentorship experiences affect the graduates and their respective ministries post-graduation?

Our research indicated that the mentoring experiences upon the graduates had the most significant effects in avoiding burnout, increased competence and confidence in teaching and preaching, study habits, and dealing with conflict management and controversial issues in ministry. We have also found that 93% of the graduates continue to serve or desire to serve in ministry. Of the participants in the study, 60% stated that their satisfaction with ministry has increased,

33% said it has remained the same, and 6% want to be doing more than they are at the present time.

(3) Did the graduates experience a mentoring relationship that was in harmony with the biblical shepherding model of spiritual leadership?

The graduates received mentoring via an informal model. On a 1 – 10 scale, the participants rated their mentoring according to the biblical shepherding model as an 8.9/10. The ratings descended from faculty (8.9), to directors (7.5 and 8.9), to members (6.8), to elders (4.9). The mentoring experiences of the participants in this case study had a tremendous impact on them while in the school of preaching and now that they are actively involved in ministry. One graduate summarized his experiences at the school by saying,

> I got the chance at school preaching to learn from some of those ministers that I've looked up to. I would say that going to the school was one of the greatest experiences of my life and getting the chance to learn and study more in-depth the Bible. So many of these men, I had such great respect for, so many of these men. I had respect for every single one of those instructors there. It was a pleasure. But it was also an honor. I felt blessed to be able to do that.

Chapter Six

Final Thoughts

How did the mentoring experiences of the graduates of the selected school of preaching affect their learning and preparation for ministry while in the respective program? In accordance with the example of Jesus who equipped His disciples for a greater purpose, taught them the value of serving others (Mark 10:44, 45), and entrusted them with the work of continuing His mission of seeking and saving the lost by preaching the gospel to the world (Matt. 28:19, 20; Mark 16:15, 16; Luke 24:47, 48; cf. Luke 19:10), we have found that these students were equipped and inspired to continue the legacy of their mentors. As did Paul with Timothy and Titus, the mentors in this school acted as shepherds, setting before the students an example of Christ-like service and sacrifice. The mentors nurtured and fed them through their teaching, while equipping and entrusting them to continue their work. Thus, in the setting of this school of preaching, the theological students benefited from having role models to provide Christian examples and mentoring relationships to direct them within their educational community.[1]

A Legacy Worth Sharing

The concept of the legacy being handed down to the students from the teachers prompted the development of the mentoring relationship. Discipleship, biblical education, and

---

[1] Chiroma, 3.

preparation for ministry resulted. The idea of belonging to, maintaining, and continuing a legacy was a theme which was unique to this study when compared to similar studies conducted for universities and seminaries. The encouragement to maintain a legacy of a faithful school of preaching and being faithful ministers of the gospel proved effective to motivate and inspire the students while in school and as graduates in ministry. The participants experienced a transparent and genuine affection from their mentors while in the school of preaching. It was expressed on multiple occasions how the school cared about their well-being, "not just their grades." The students, in turn, also seemed to place a greater emphasis on truly learning the Bible and being faithful to the word than on scoring highly on tests, papers, etc. The students wanted to score highly, but it does not appear that grades were more important than genuinely learning the text.

The participants were also encouraged, motivated, and inspired by the work ethic of their mentors. Graduates saw the time and effort put into their classes while also realizing these teachers were dedicated to fulltime ministry in churches of Christ. Moreover, as the participants came to value the sacrifices of their teachers, their recognition of the need for selflessness and service in ministry increased. They were humbled by the sacrifices their teachers were willing to make for them. They came to appreciate the efforts being taken to ensure they were taught and prepared for ministry. Many of the teachers were driving from 3 to 4 hours in distance to teach at the school. Most of the teachers were not fulltime faculty members, meaning they received only a small stipend for their work. While the distance they traveled had an adverse effect on the amount of time some teachers were able to spend with the students, the sacrifices they made to be teaching at the school did not go unnoticed. Such recognition and appreciation, in turn, motivated greater effort and developed a greater understanding for learning in the scholastic environment of the school of preaching. Being motivated by the responsibility of continuing a legacy and the sacrificial efforts of their teachers, the students became even more determined to succeed and to please their mentors.

How did these mentorship experiences affect the graduates and their respective ministries post-graduation? The participants believe they are part of a legacy. The concept of being part of a legacy motivated them to take ownership in the school and to maintain the work they were doing by taking their studies seriously. Through the shared legacy of the school, the students recognized they were part of something bigger than themselves and strove to make their unique contribution to the betterment of the learning environment they were provided. The encouragement to maintain the legacy of their mentors also proved effective to motivate and inspire the students as graduates in ministry. The students believe their respective ministries are a continuation of the ministerial legacies of their mentors.

The participants also saw the need for organization and structure in their lives through the example of their mentors. By emulating the work ethic of their mentors, the participants believe they are better prepared to meet the time and work requirements in fulltime ministry.

The legacy they hope to continue is one of "sound doctrine" and "biblical preaching." Time and again the participants spoke of their regard for the "truth" and their responsibility to preach the truth. The graduates have come to realize that their efforts in preaching are not just about style, taste, or preference. They also seem to understand the difference in preaching opinions and hobbies instead of the Bible. The participants indicated their appreciation for preaching the word of God as a matter of authority, recognizing that human opinion lacks the same authority as biblical revelation. For the participants, the legacy of their mentors is one of biblical preaching and conveys the message of Christ as authorized by God. The legacy which the graduates hope to maintain is one which is known for content-oriented preaching, which is judged for its use of scripture and faithfulness to the word.

The participants also do not convey any sense of hesitancy to avoid preaching sermons that might be deemed controversial. Christian evidences, ethics, and morality were given considerable time and attention in the school. The graduates admired the ability of their mentors to defend the existence of God, Deity of Christ, and inspiration of the Bible. Likewise, they believe they are better prepared to defend the Christian religion in an increasingly secular society. Our findings agree that when theological training is coupled with effective mentoring in these schools, the spiritual growth, character development, and ministry formation of the students will be enhanced.[2]

The Shepherd Leadership Model

Did the graduates experience a mentoring relationship that was in harmony with the biblical shepherding model of spiritual leadership? The school which provided our case study mentors effectively without a formal mentoring program or structure. We have found that in the school of preaching setting a formal mentoring program does not necessarily have to be in place for effective mentoring to occur. The school under consideration offered no formal mentoring sessions, programs, or activities, but this did not seem to deter mentoring from occurring. On this point, our findings seem to contradict those of previous studies, wherein it has been stated, "Schools accomplish their desired goal by providing a setting or program in which the mentoring experience can thrive and wherein comprehensive orientation and training for mentors is provided."[3]

At this particular school of preaching, no comprehensive orientation and mentor training is offered to the teachers. Our study does not suggest that these things are unnecessary in every setting; however, in this setting, where teachers mentored with spiritual maturity, biblical knowledge, and by implementing the biblical model of shepherd leadership, comprehensive training and orientation for structured mentoring was not essential to being effective.

---

[2] Chiroma, 1.
[3] Kretzschmar, 8.

In the case of this school, the effectiveness for mentoring has been developed through an understanding and implementation of the biblical shepherd model of spiritual leadership. While a setting for effective informal mentoring is in place, no program of formal mentoring exists. Yet, the participants rated the mentoring environment 7.6/10; they rated the mentoring received 8.9/10; and their satisfaction with the mentoring they received has increased since graduation for 88.8% of the participants in this study.

Mentoring effectiveness was made possible through small class sizes and from mentors making themselves available and accessible after classes concluded. We concur with Mwangi's research which showed that the transformative process is impacted through dialogue and relationship building and from sharing thoughts and experiences.[4] Our findings show that dialogue and relationship building were a greater contributing factor to the healthy mentoring experience than any formal structures or models which might have been designed.

The mentoring model at the school of preaching was informal, greatly appreciated, and highly effective. On a 1 – 10 scale, the participants rated their mentoring according to the biblical shepherding model as an 8.9/10. The ratings descended from faculty (8.9), to directors (7.5 and 8.9), to members (6.8), to elders (4.9). The mentoring experiences of the participants in this case study had a tremendous impact on them while in the school of preaching and now that they are actively involved in ministry.

---

[4] Mwangi, 353.

We have also found that the mentoring received by the participants has aided them and prepared them to address controversial issues in ministry. This finding also agrees with similar studies which have recognized that students who have been mentored while in school also tend to have a better grasp of controversial issues in ministry, conflict management, and sermon preparation and delivery, which helped prepare them for their work in ministry.[5]

We were especially interested to find the biblical model of shepherd leadership was the primary mentoring model utilized in the school. In this model, the transparent and genuine affection exhibited for the Lord's people (in this case, the students) by the leader (in this case, the teachers, director, elders, and church members) provided a truer indication of a shepherd leader than the ministry techniques utilized.[6]

Relationships between teachers and students were essential to the moral formation of the students. The moral formation of the students was enhanced through a combination of strong directive leadership, elements of collaboration, elements of participation, and elements of apprenticeship leading to the spiritual transformation of the disciples.[7] We found mentors in this school who directed the students and helped them to navigate a faithful course in the world, offering direction while following the lead of the Good Shepherd.

---

[5] Strunk, 537–50.
[6] Gunter, 10.
[7] Walton, 41.

The graduates were mentored in the classroom and in an informal setting which naturally occurred from time spent outside the classroom. Therefore, we found that whether mentoring occurs in a structured mentoring environment or organically, a school of preaching can encourage spiritual and character formation, while also developing sound leadership characteristics in the students. We found that the mentors who served as shepherds to the students, desired to help, and led the students to become servants as well. By serving the students, the mentors imitated the shepherd leadership of Christ. The mentors became active participants in the ministry of the school of preaching by serving as pedagogical models of proper behavior and desires.[8] The mentors came to be appreciated as leaders who desired to see their students involved in the ministry and mission of Christ and to use their talents and abilities to fulfill their respective ministries and thereby bring glory to God.

However, one of the greatest possible obstacles to effective mentoring in theological education is that a mentor could be overworked.[9] Our study also validated this concern as it was repeatedly suggested by the participants that one of their primary mentors, the school's director, was being overworked.

Implications

From the findings above, implications gathered from this research will begin with the issue of the workload of the director. The participants in our study repeatedly suggested

---

[8] Lamb, 203.
[9] Chiroma, 6.

that one of their primary mentors in the school of preaching was the school's director. Yet, they were fearful that he was being overworked and overstressed by attempting to fulfill two fulltime jobs, i.e. the school's fulltime director and a career in fulltime ministry. If his health failed, his absence could prove to be detrimental to the mentoring of future students.

Our study also indicated the effectiveness of having experienced evangelists training the forthcoming generations of evangelists. In this school, men have been employed who have a reputation for faithfully preaching the gospel regardless of academic notoriety. While this school does not belittle academic credentials for their teachers, academic credentials are not the primary concern for the elders or the director when selecting faculty members. Rather, the credentials of having a reputation and regard for knowledge of the Christian Scriptures, faithfulness in churches of Christ, and a proven track record in ministry are most important when choosing faculty members for this school. The school has chosen to hire mature, knowledgeable, and faithful gospel preachers to reproduce themselves in the lives of their students. This course seems most prudent and effective for a school of preaching.

Some of the participants spoke of a perceived deficiency in the evangelistic program of the school. Evangelistic campaigns were also recommended by a couple of participants as a solution. It was said by multiple participants that their education in New Testament Greek has not proven to be as practical and necessary in ministry as were the courses in evangelism. As schools of preaching are being relied upon more and more for ministry training in churches of Christ, and considering the decline in churches of Christ in the United States in recent years, it would seem imperative to the effectiveness, influence, and legacy of any school of preaching to prioritize personal evangelism and practical theology.

The "hands on" approach and in-depth interviews conducted by the elders with prospective students seems to be quite prudent and necessary. The elders recognize that not every prospective student is qualified or ready to be a student in a school of preaching, especially one whose program of study is intense and demanding. The selective approach to student enrolment on the part of the elders could also be a significant factor for the high percentage of graduates still active in ministry. The elders appear to accept into the program only those who are serious about learning the curriculum and serving in ministry.

Having taught in schools of preaching since 2003, and speaking from experience, not every eldership which oversees a school of preaching has this practice; however, this research has indicated the wisdom in so doing. Not every prospective student belongs in a school of preaching, especially a fulltime program. As the participants have expressed, these programs are designed to be intensive. Success in such a program and in fulltime ministry demands a certain quality of mind, work ethic, and zeal for ministry.

One final implication from this study is the need for greater relationships to be built and maintained between the students and the elders and members of the hosting congregation. As our study has indicated, the relationships do not necessarily have to be built through the development of a structured program. Being cognizant of the need and spending time with the students will do much to impact and enhance their mentoring experiences while in the school. By taking upon themselves the role of shepherd leaders for the students, the members and elders could be even more instrumental in the mentoring experiences of the students.

Recommendations for Future Research

Upon completing the research study, we can generate several recommendations that can be used by future researchers and scholars who are planning to conduct a similar study. The first recommendation for future research pertaining to the mentoring experiences in schools of preaching operated by churches of Christ is to focus on mentoring from the perspective of the leadership of the schools. It would be fruitful to learn about the mentoring relationships in schools of preaching from the perspective of the faculty. Is there a certain demographic or quality of student that makes for a better mentee than others? Is a structured mentoring program feasible in schools of preaching? What training or experience should the faculty have in formal mentoring and leadership education? What are they doing to encourage a sense of legacy among their students? Interviews could also be conducted with directors of schools of preaching with some of the same questions in mind. Interviewing elders could also contribute to a multi-faceted examination of leadership in schools of preaching in general.

A second recommendation for future study of schools of preaching could be an expansion to include the wives of preaching school students. What effects do these programs have on the families of the students? Have marriages ended in part because of the time required to undertake intensified and exhaustive studies in a school of preaching? What effect does life in a school of preaching have on the finances of a family? How can healthy mentoring experiences alleviate some of these burdens and provide spiritual guidance to the family?

A third recommendation for future research would be to offer a comparative study among the various schools of preaching affiliated with churches of Christ. How do the mentoring practices compare from "School A" to "School B"? Research could discover data from among the schools in ministry retention, job efficacy, conflict management in ministry, etc.

Final Thoughts

Churches of Christ rely greatly upon schools of preaching to assist in the training of minsters. If spiritual leaders are to come from these schools, these schools of preaching must have genuine spiritual leaders to shepherd them. The schools will need men who exercise their values and personal growth to lead the students in ways which edify and enable them to achieve spiritual growth. By leading from the standpoint of true, biblical, and spiritual values, those who are led will be able to recognize that their leaders are genuinely concerned with their eternal well-being as well as their happiness in life.

Schools of preaching must have shepherd leaders. The men entrusted with training forthcoming generations of evangelists must be faithful to the work of ministry and to the Chief Shepherd of our souls. The relationship among the students and their mentors in the schools of preaching must be built upon trust, shared values, and shared goals. By embracing shared values, and working toward common goals, spiritual maturity and transformation can be achieved. Students in these schools must have men who have a transparent and genuine affection exhibited for them. The students entering these schools should desire and expect to find mentors who would encourage spiritual transformation through participation and a developed relationship.[10] Students should expect to find a mentoring experience based upon the common goal and the shared values of preaching the gospel, edifying the church, and saving the lost.[11] The students should expect to grow spiritually as they imitate the faith of their teachers.[12]

As our study has also indicated, sometimes an effective mentoring experience requires "unlearning" certain things detrimental to the spiritual growth process on the part of the mentee. The student should expect to find encouragement to learn, grow, and persevere, as well as to unlearn bad habits and retrain his thinking when necessary.[13] The schools of preaching need shepherd leaders who are keenly interested and actively involved in the growth and health of the

---
[10] Shepherd, 99.
[11] Bartlett, 32.
[12] Lamb, 189–207.
[13] Currie, 47.

students. The work these schools seek to undertake is too important to require anything less than the biblical shepherd leadership model. The viability of these schools to offer suitable ministerial training depends upon their awareness and ability to provide a biblical mentoring experience to their students.

Being part of a legacy is a theme which is unique to these findings when compared to similar studies conducted for universities and seminaries. For a legacy to be maintained it must be valued and respected. The mentors in this school are respected by the mentees for their knowledge, character, work ethic, sacrifice, and faithfulness. The qualities of the mentors are admirable to the mentees. The mentors are held in high esteem. Knowing that their mentors care genuinely for them only enhances the learning experience and ministry preparation of the students.

Let us now conclude by offering a personal observation. In our opinion. this study has highlighted a school worthy of our appreciation and affection. We have personally come to appreciate this school for the tremendous success it has had over the last ten years by coupling a Bible-based program with Bible-based mentoring. In the school of preaching which we have evaluated, the Bible was at the heart of the program. The Bible was in the heart of the curriculum. The Bible was in the heart of the teachers, the directors, the elders, and the members of the hosting congregation. The result, the Bible is now in the hearts of its graduates, their ministries, and their future. To God be the glory!

Interview Questions

1. What is your understanding of the responsibilities of the mentor and of the one being mentored in the mentoring relationship?

2. Having graduated from a school of preaching, please describe your ideal environment for mentoring in a school of preaching setting based upon your experiences? Using a scale of 1 to 10, (1 being very poor and 10 being ideal) how do your mentoring experiences while in school rate according to your ideal model?

3. Please provide examples of how your school contributed to an ideal mentoring environment. If you do not believe your school contributed to an ideal mentoring environment, please explain.

4. Using a scale of 1 to 10, (1 being very poor and 10 being ideal) how do the elders of the host congregation rate in their mentoring of you as a student according to your ideal model? Please provide an example of how the elders of the congregation who oversaw the school contributed to an ideal mentoring environment. If you do not believe the elders of the overseeing congregation significantly contributed to providing an ideal mentoring environment, please explain.

5. Would you describe the mentoring environment as being more formal and structured or informal and naturally experienced through relationships that developed over time? Using a scale of structured or unstructured (1 being

very unstructured and 10 being very structured) how would you rate your mentoring experiences?

6. Was there sufficient informal time with the faculty to build good relationships (1 being very insufficient and 10 being very sufficient)? How much time per week do you estimate that you were able to talk with your mentors outside of class? 0-1 hour__ 1-2 hours__ 2-3 hours__ other__

7. How did the informal time spent with faculty affect the professional relationship often maintained between teachers and students?

8. What positive qualities or traits were gained from your mentor(s)?

9. Could you describe one event where you are more effective as a minister because of what you learned from your mentors while in school?

10. Using a scale of 1 to 10, (1 being very poor and 10 being ideal) how did the director of the school rate according to your ideal model? Please provide examples of how the director of the school contributed to providing an ideal mentoring environment. If you believe the director did not contribute significantly to an ideal mentoring environment, please explain.

11. Using a scale of 1 to 10, (1 being very poor and 10 being ideal) how did the members of the congregation rate according to your ideal model? Please provide an example of how the members of the overseeing congregation contributed to providing an ideal mentoring environment.

If you do not believe the members of the congregation contributed significantly to your mentoring experiences, please explain.

12. Looking back, how did your mentoring experiences contribute to your learning and preparation for ministry while you were in the program? Consider your grades, retention of the subjects studied, recommended books for your ministerial library, advice given, recommendation for ministry and ministerial opportunities, and relationships developed, etc.

13. How did these mentoring experiences contribute to your respective ministry post-graduation? Consider tenure, job efficacy, confidence, burnout, etc. If you do not believe these experiences contributed significantly to your post-graduation ministry, please explain.

14. Using a scale of 1 to 10, (1 being very poor and 10 being ideal) how would you rate the effectiveness of your mentoring experiences upon your ministry post-graduation?

15. Would you say you experienced a mentoring experience that was in harmony with the biblical shepherding model of spiritual leadership? How many biblical mentors do you suppose you had in school?

16. First rank from 1-10 (1 being poor and 10 being excellent) and then describe your satisfaction or lack thereof with the mentoring model you experienced.

17. Has your satisfaction with the mentoring you experienced in school increased or decreased over time?

18. Have the mentoring relationships which began in school increased or decreased over time?

19. Has your satisfaction with ministry 1) increased; 2) decreased; or 3) remained constant over time?

20. How did your mentoring experiences with the school contribute to your ability and willingness to mentor others?

References

Adams, Christopher J., Holly Hough, Rae Proeschold-bell, Jia Yao, and Melanie Kolkin. "Clergy Burnout: A Comparison Study with Other Helping Professions." *Pastoral Psychology* 66, no. 2 (April 2017): 147–175.

Anekstein, Alyse M., and Linwood G. Vereen. "Research Mentoring: A Study of Doctoral Student Experiences and Research Productivity." *Journal of Counselor Preparation and Supervision* 11, no. 1 (2018): 1–28.

Anshel, Mark H., and Mitchell Smith. "The Role of Religious Leaders in Promoting Healthy Habits in Religious Institutions." *Journal of Religion and Health* 53, no. 4 (2014): 1046–1059.

Bartlett, David L. "Mentoring in the New Testament." In *Mentoring: Biblical, Theological, and Practical Perspectives*, edited by Dean k. Thompson and D. Cameron Murchison, 23–36. Grand Rapids, MI: Eerdmans Publishing Company, 2018.

Bauer, Walter. *A Greek English Lexicon of the New Testament and Other Early Christian Literature*, edited by Fredrick William Danker, third edition. Chicago: Chicago University Press, 2000.

Beale, G.K., and D.A. Carson. *Commentary on the New Testament Use of the Old Testament*. Grand Rapids, MI: Baker Academic, 2007.

Beard, Christopher B. "Connecting Spiritual Formation and Adult Learning Theory: An Examination of Common Principles." *Christian Education Journal* 14, no. 2 (Fall 2017): 247–269.

Beasley-Murray, George R. *John*. Word Biblical Commentary; Nashville, TN: Thomas Nelson Publishers, 1999.

Bell, Robert S. "An Elder's Charge." *Firm Foundation* 96, no. 1 (January 79): 52.

Block, Daniel I. *The Book of Ezekiel: Chapters 25–48*. New International Commentary of the Old Testament; Grand Rapids, MI: Eerdmans Publishing Company, 1998.

Boswell, Jennifer, Marcella D. Stark, Angie D. Wilson, and Anthony J. Onwuegbuzie. "The Impact of Dual Roles in Mentoring Relationships: A Mixed Research Study." *Journal of Counselor Preparation and Supervision* 9, no. 2 (2017): 1–27.

Breed, Gert. "The *Diakonia* of the Elders according to 1 Peter." *Die Skriflig* 50, no. 3 (August 2016): 1–8.

Brown, Francis, S.R. Driver, Charles A. Briggs, and Wilhelm Gensenius, *The New Brown, Driver, Briggs, Gensenius Hebrew and English Lexicon*. Lafayette, IN: Associated Publishers and Authors, 1978.

Bruce, F.F. *The Book of Acts*, revised edition. New International Commentary of the New Testament; Grand Rapids, MI: Eerdmans Publishing Company, 1988.

Brueggemann, Walter. "Mentoring in the Old Testament." In *Mentoring: Biblical, Theological, and Practical Perspectives*, edited by Dean K. Thompson and D. Cameron Murchison, 7–22. Grand Rapids, MI: Eerdmans Publishing Company, 2018.

Bushfield, Timothy. "Teaching with Trajectory: Equipping Students for the Lifelong Journey of Learning to Preach." In *Training Preachers: A Guide to Teaching Homiletics*, edited by Scott M. Gibson, 164–87. Bellingham, WA: Lexham Press, 2018.

Carson, D.A. *The Gospel According to John.* Pillar New Testament Commentary; Grand Rapids, MI: Eerdmans Publishing Company, 1991.

Chandler, Diane J. "Whole-Person Formation: An Integrative Approach to Christian Education." *Christian Education Journal* 12, no. 2 (Fall 2015): 314–332.

Chiroma, Nathan H., and Anita Cloete. "Mentoring as a Supportive Pedagogy in Theological Training." *Hervormde Teologiese Studies* 71, no. 3 (2015): 1–8.

Clinton, J. Robert. *Titus: Apostolic Leadership*. Altadena, CA: Barnabas Publishers, 2001.

Creswell John W., and Cheryl N. Poth, *Qualitative Inquiry and Research Design: Choosing Among Five Approaches*, fourth, ed., Thousand Oaks, CA: SAGE Publications, 2018.

Currie, Thomas W. "Theological-Pastoral Perspectives on Mentoring." In *Mentoring: Biblical, Theological, and Practical Perspectives*, edited by Dean K. Thompson and D. Cameron Murchison, 39–54. Grand Rapids, MI: Eerdmans Publishing Company, 2018.

Dale, Robert D., *Pastoral Leadership*. Nashville, TN: Abingdon Press, 2001.

——— *Seeds for the Future: Growing Organic Leaders for Living Churches*. St. Louis, MO: Lake Hickory Resources, 2005.

——— *To Dream Again, Again*. Macon, GA: Nurturing Faith, Inc., 2018.

Dempster, Stephen G. *Dominion and Dynasty: A Theology of the Hebrew Bible*. Downers Grove, IL: IVP Apollos, 2003.

Evans, Jean. "Experience and Convergence in Spiritual Direction." *Journal of Religion and Health* 54 no. 1 (February 2015): 264–278.

Fair, Ian, A., *Leadership in the Kingdom: Sensitive Strategies for the Church in a Changing World*. Abilene, TX: ACU Press, 2008.

Fairholm, Gilbert. *Capturing the Heart of Leadership: Spirituality and Community in the New American Workplace*. Westport, CT: Greenwood Publishing Group, 2000.

Fruiht, Veronica, and Thomas Chan. "Naturally Occurring Mentorship in a National Sample of First-Generation

College Goers: A Promising Portal for Academic and Developmental Success." *American Journal of Community Psychology* 61, no. 3 (June 2018): 386–397.

Fuhr, Richard Alan Jr., and Gary E. Yates. *The Message of the Twelve*. Nashville, TN: B&H Academic, 2016.

Gambrell, Mary Latimer. *Ministerial Training in Eighteenth-Century New England*. New York: American Missionary Society, 1967.

Gibson, Scott M. "The Place of Preaching Professors in Theological Education." In *Training Preachers: A Guide to Teaching Homiletics*, edited by Scott M. Gibson, 5–23. Bellingham, WA: Lexham Press, 2018.

Gunter, Nathan H. "For the Flock: Impetus for Shepherd Leadership in John 10." *The Journal of Applied Christian Leadership* 10, no. 1 (Spring 2016): 8–18.

Hancock, Dawson R., and Bob Algozzine. *Doing Case Study Research: A Practical Guide for Beginning Researchers*. Teachers College Press, 2016.

Harris, R. Laird, Gleason L. Archer, Jr., and Bruce K. Waltke, *Theological Wordbook of the Old Testament*. Chicago: Moody Publishers, 1980.

Harp, Scott. *The Sage of Jasper: Gus Nichols, A Biography*. Charleston, AR: Cobb Publishing, 2019.

Hartwig, Ryan T., and Warren Bird. *Teams that Thrive: Five Disciplines of Collaborative Church Leadership.* Downers Grove, IL: Inter-Varsity Press, 2015.

Hearn, Roy J. "Getwell Road School of Preaching." *Gospel Advocate* 110, no. 5 (February 1968): 68.

——— "Wanted: Men Who Are Not Afraid of Hard Work," *First Century Christian* 1, no.4 (October 1967): 9–10.

Henry-Noel, Nayanee, Maria Bishop, Clement K. Gwede, Ekaterina Petkova, and Ewa Szumacher. "Mentorship in Medicine and Other Health Professions." *Journal of Cancer Education* 33, no. 2 (April 2018): 1–9.

Hengstenberg, E.W. *Christology of the Old Testament*. Grand Rapids, MI: Kregel Publications, 1970.

Highers, Alan E. "Getwell Road School of Preaching." *Gospel Advocate* 108, no. 5 (February 1966): 68.

Hogan, Norman. *Leadership in the Local Church.* Henderson, TN: Hester Publications, 1988.

Holliday, William L. *A Concise Hebrew and Aramaic Lexicon of the Old Testament*. Grand Rapids, MI: Eerdmans Publishing Company, 1988.

Kittel, Gerhard ed. "*poimēn*." In *Theological Dictionary of the New Testament*, vol. 6, trans. Geoffrey W. Bromiley. Grand Rapids, MI: Eerdmans, 1984.

Klink III, Edward W. *John*. Zondervan Exegetical Commentary of the New Testament; Grand Rapids, MI: Zondervan, 2016.

Kretzschmar, Louise, and Ethel C. Tuckey. "The Role of Relationship in Moral Formation: An Analysis of Three Tertiary Theological Education Institutions in South Africa." *Die Skriflig* 51, no. 1 (2017): 1–8.

Lamb, Gregory E. "Saint Peter as 'Sympresbyteros': Mimetic Desire, Discipleship, and Education." *Christian Education Journal* 15, no. 2 (2018): 189–207.

Laniak, Timothy S. *Shepherds after My Own Heart: Pastoral Traditions and Leadership in the Bible*. Downers Grove, IL: Inter-Varsity Press, 2006.

Lemke, Dale L. "The Philosophy of Disciple-Centered Leadership," *Christian Education Journal* 14, no. 2 (2017): 271–284.

Lemmons, Ruel. "Bear Valley Opens School of Preaching." *Firm Foundation* 82, no. 27 (July 1965): 427.

———. "The Training of Gospel Preachers." *Firm Foundation* 82, no. 27 (July 1965): 418.

Lindholm, Greg, Judy Johnston, Frank Dong, Kim Moore, and Elizabeth Ablah. "Clergy Wellness: An Assessment of Perceived Barriers to Achieving Healthier Lifestyles." *Journal of Religion and Health* 55, no. 1 (February 2016): 97–109.

McMaster, Jeffrey S. "The Influence of Christian Education on Leadership Development." *The Journal of Applied Christian Leadership* 7, no. 1 (Spring 2013): 68–84.

Michaels, J. Ramsey. *The Gospel of John.* New International Commentary of the New Testament; Grand Rapids, MI: Eerdmans Publishing Company, 2010.

Mounce, William D. *Pastoral Epistles.* Word Biblical Commentary; Nashville, TN: Thomas Nelson Publishers, 2000.

Mwangi, Mary Wanjiru. "Perspective Transformation through Small Group Discipleship among Undergraduate University Students in Nairobi, Kenya." *Christian Education Journal* 15, no. 3 (December 2018): 340–360.

Muschallik, Julia, and Kerstin Pull. "Mentoring in Higher Education: Does It Enhance Mentees' Research Productivity?" *Education Economics* 24, no. 2 (January 1, 2016): 210–23.

Nwanzu, Chiyem L. "Academic Programme Satisfaction and Doctorate Aspiration among Master's Degree Students: The Role of Mentoring Experience." *Ife Psychologia* 25, no. 1 (March 2017): 424–443.

Payne, J. Barton. *Encyclopedia of Biblical Prophecy.* New York: Harper and Row Publishers, 1973.

Puls, Timothy R., Laverne L. Ludden, and James Freemyer. "Authentic Leadership and Its Relationship to Ministerial

Effectiveness." *The Journal of Applied Christian Leadership* 8, no. 1 (Spring 2014): 55–75.

Resane, K. Thomas. "Leadership in the Church: The Shepherd Model." *Hervormde Teologiese Studies* 70, no. 1 (May 2014): 1–6.

Robinson, Edward J. *Show Us How You Do It: Marshall Keeble and the rise of Black Churches of Christ in the United States, 1914-1968*. Tuscaloosa, AL: University of Alabama Press, 2008.

Royster, Carl. *Churches of Christ in the United States*. Nashville, TN: 21st Century Christian, 2018.

Ryken, Leland, James C. Wilhoit, Tremper Longman III. "Sheep, Shepherd." In *Dictionary of Biblical Imagery* (Downers Grove, IL Inter-Varsity Press, 1998), 782.

Shepherd, Roger E., *Church Growth and Membership Involvement in a Contemporary Community*. Montgomery, AL: Amridge University Press, 2018.

Silva, Moises, ed. *The New International Dictionary of New Testament Theology and Exegesis*, rev. ed., vol.4. Grand Rapids, MI: Zondervan, 2014.

Sparkman, Torrence E. "The Leadership Development Experiences of Church Denomination Executives." *The Journal of Applied Christian Leadership* 11, no. 1 (Spring 2017): 54–68.

Strunk, Joshua, Frederick Milacci, and James Zabloski. "The Convergence of Ministry, Tenure, and Efficacy: Beyond Speculation Toward a New Theory of Pastoral Efficacy." *Pastoral Psychology* 66, no. 4 (August 2017): 537–550.

Swinton, John. *Practical Theology and Qualitative Research*, London: Hymns Ancient & Modern Ltd, 2006.

Taylor, John B. *Ezekiel: An Introduction and Commentary*. Tyndale Old Testament Commentary; Downers Grove, IL: Inter-Varsity Press, 1969.

Vaughan, Matthew Emile. "On Schools of Preaching." *Journal of Faith and Academy* 5, no. 1 (Spring 2012): 60–74.

Walton, John H. *Old Testament Theology for Christians: From Ancient Context to Enduring Belief.* Downers Grove, IL: IVP Academic, 2017.

White, Peter, and Samuel K. Afrane. "Maintaining Christian Virtues and Ethos in Christian Universities in Ghana: The Reality, Challenges and the Way Forward." *Hervormde Teologiese Studies* 73, no. 3 (2017): 1–8.

Williamson, W. P., and Ralph W. Hood. "The Role of Mentoring in Spiritual Transformation: A Faith-Based Approach to Recovery from Substance Abuse." *Pastoral Psychology* 64, no. 1 (February 2015): 135–152.

Willimon, William H. *Pastor: The Theology and Practice of Ordained Ministry*. Nashville, TN: Abingdon Press, 2016.

Wilson, William. *Wilson's Old Testament Word Studies*. Peabody, MA: Hendrickson Publishers, 1993.

Wright, Christopher J.H. *Knowing Jesus through the Old Testament*. Downers Grove, IL: IVP Academic, 2014.

Yarbrough, Robert W. *The Letters to Timothy and Titus*. Pillar New Testament Commentary; Grand Rapids, MI: Eerdmans Publishing Company, 2018.